Outdoor Gas Griddle Grill Cookbook 1000

The Complete Guide with Easy Tasty Effortless Griddle Grilling Recipes for Anyone Who Wants to Have An Amazing Taste Bud

By Grace Jason

Legal & Disclaimer

The information contained in this book and its contents is not designed to replace or take the place of any form of medical or professional advice; and is not meant to replace the need for independent medical, financial, legal or other professional advice or services, as may be required. The content and information in this book has been provided for educational and entertainment purposes only.

The content and information contained in this book has been compiled from sources deemed reliable, and it is accurate to the best of the Author's knowledge, information and belief. However, the Author cannot guarantee its accuracy and validity and cannot be held liable for any errors and/or omissions. Further, changes are periodically made to this book as and when needed. Where appropriate and/or necessary, you must consult a professional (including but not limited to your doctor, attorney, financial advisor or such other professional advisor) before using any of the suggested remedies, techniques, or information in this book.

Upon using the contents and information contained in this book, you agree to hold harmless the Author from and against any damages, costs, and expenses, including any legal fees potentially resulting from the application of any of the information provided by this book. This disclaimer applies to any loss, damages or injury caused by the use and application, whether directly or indirectly, of any advice or information presented, whether for breach of contract, tort, negligence, personal injury, criminal intent, or under any other cause of action.

You agree to accept all risks of using the information presented inside this book.

You agree that by continuing to read this book, where appropriate and/or necessary, you shall consult a professional (including but not limited to your doctor, attorney, or financial advisor or such other advisor as needed) before using any of the suggested remedies, techniques, or information in this book.

Table of Contents

Description

A thousand-year-old preservation strategy, smoking is a tribal method that gives lovely taste and unrivaled delicacy to food. It is additionally a binding together method of cooking that requires painstakingness and persistence, yet over every one of the unfathomable energy for good food.

This book is the sensible continuation of this extraordinary experience, a genuine authoritative manual for the flame broiling room on account of which we need to demystify and make this lovely cooking instrument much progressively open.

Would you like to begin picking up interesting frying pan barbecuing, yet you don't know where to begin? Pondering which smoker to purchase, how to light and keep up a fire, how to smoke hot and cold, or what wood to utilize?

Presently you can without much of a stretch barbecue your preferred meat, vegetables and appreciate it easily.

In this book you will get to know:

- Fundamentals of Griddle Grilling
- Tips and Tricks of Griddle Grilling
- Common FAQs of Griddle Grilling
- Recipes for Breakfast
- Poultry
- Fish and Seafood
- Pork
- Beef
- Game Recipes

And Much More..

For any individual who wants to cook outside: These plans are exceptionally composed for cooking on any model of open air level top iron.

This book contains all the basic strategies to ace your griddle grill plans like an ace just as 80 Easy and Delicious Griddle Grill fundamental plans for cooking the best meat, the most heavenly barbecued fish, yet additionally a wide range of different nourishments, for example, fish, vegetables and even bites!

With the correct instruments and the correct information, you will see that the craft of smoking is a lot easier than it appears. It is safe to say that you are prepared to turn into an ace smoker?

The most heavenly of smoked fish, yet in addition a wide range of different nourishments, similar to cheeses, vegetables and even bread! With the correct devices and the correct information, you will see that the craft of smoking is a lot.

What are you waiting for? Let's start!

Introduction

The Blackstone Flat Top Griddle provides 720 inches of professional grade griddle for your back yard or really anywhere you go. Now, you can make professional quality meals and get the same results professional chefs achieve every time you cook. Make eggs, pancakes, quesadillas, grilled cheese, steak, potatoes, teppanyaki style foods and more. The Blackstone Flat Top Griddle is designed to produce perfectly even and adjustable heat over four different cooking zones, so you can always have the exact temperature you need at a moment's notice.

The Blackstone Flat Top Griddle is made with professional grade materials and provides professional quality heat in the form of 60,000 BTU of cooking power with four independent cooking zones. This means you can carefully control everything you cook with individual controls for each zone. Eggs don't cook properly at the same temperature as a steak, and the Blackstone Griddle allows you to cook both, perfectly, at the same time.

Are you an avid camper? Do you love to tailgate before the big game? Do you like to cook at friends' houses? Well, the Blackstone Griddle allows you maximum flexibility by letting you take your griddle wherever you need to go. With minimal effort you can remove the flat top, safely fold and stow the legs, and remove the propane tank. Best of all, the griddle comes with industrial grade casters so you can roll the griddle wherever it needs to go.

Because it's built from industrial grade materials, your Blackstone Griddle will be a versatile appliance for many years to come. The frame of the griddle is built with super durable powder coated steel. The burners are made from restaurant grade stainless steel and are guaranteed to produce perfectly even and powerful heat for years to come. Once you've spent some time with your Blackstone Griddle you might even consider getting rid of your more conventional gas or charcoal grills.

Say goodbye to dirty charcoal and matches forever. Charcoal is dirty, expensive, and harmful to your health, so why are you still using it? The Blackstone Griddle uses a standard refillable propane tank which attaches to the griddle with ease. And thanks to the simple push button ignitor, starting your griddle is as easy as pushing a button.

Chapter 1: Fundamentals of Griddle Grilling

What is Griddle Grill?

You may not be surprised to hear that grilling food is a pretty old technique. In fact, it goes back over a half a million years. Early humans found that meat cooked over fire was actually more nutritious than raw meat.

What's the reason?

Bioavailability, in short, cooking meat changes the structure of proteins and fats allowing them to be more efficiently digested and absorbed by the body. Until the 1940s grilling was mostly something that people did around campfires, but after World War II and the expansion of suburbs, the popularity of backyard grilling skyrocketed. By the 1950s the back yard BBQ was a staple of family entertaining, and it remains this way today.

Better Than Conventional Grills?

Since the invention of the burger, the debate has raged over whether a grill or a flat top griddle does the best job. While it's true that grills offer burgers a smokier flavor, does that really result in a better burger? After years of research burger experts reached the conclusion that the flat top griddle is actually superior to the grill for one simple reason: It allows the burger to cook in its own juices rather that have all of those juices fall through the grate and into the fire. The end result is a more evenly cooked, juicier, more flavorful burger.

Modern Gas Griddles

When most people think of griddles they either picture a small counter top griddle that you plug in, or a giant flat top that sits in the kitchen of a diner. Because the griddle is so perfect for cooking such a wide variety of foods, the invention of the modern gas griddle makes perfect sense. By marrying the idea of a propane grill with the cooking surface of a griddle, you get an appliance that is both versatile and portable.

Components of Blackstone Griddle Grill

The Blackstone Griddle features an easy to use ignition system, but if you find that the ignition burner is not lighting there are several possible causes. First, check to see if the battery in the ignitor has enough power. If that is not the problem, make sure you have enough gas in the tank. Another problem may be a clogged burner or gas jet. Because food or other debris can fall into the burners, they may become clogged over time. If this is the case, remove the cooking surface and use a damp sponge to clean out the burners or gas jets.

Some users have noticed that the grease drain can allow grease to drip out of the trough and down the leg of the grill, which can cause grease to pool on the ground. In order to combat this, make sure the grease trough and the catch can are properly aligned. Misalignment can cause leaks. Also, make sure to monitor the grease level so that it does not overflow or overwhelm the grease drain. Be mindful of bits of food that may fall into the grease trough as these may also cause the grease drain to become clogged.

1. Ignition button: The battery controlled ignition button lights your griddle. Simply press, hold, and the left most burner will light.
2. Left Burner Knob: Turn clockwise to control the heat on the left burner.
3. Left-Center Burner Knob: Turn clockwise to increase the heat on the left-center burner.
4. Right-Center Burner Knob: Turn clockwise to increase the heat on the right-center burner.
5. Right Burner Knob: Turn clockwise to increase the heat on the right burner.

If you find that food sticks to the surface of the griddle, there are several causes with simple solutions. First, you may not have properly seasoned the griddle. Because the griddle does not come pre-seasoned you should be sure to do this before using. Your food may also stick because you are adding it to the griddle too soon. Since the heavy cooking surface needs a little time to heat up, make sure that it is at the proper temperature before adding food. You can do this by touching a corner or small piece of food to the griddle. If it immediately sticks, wait another few minutes. Another common cause of food sticking to the griddle, is not giving it enough time to cook. Great chefs know that you shouldn't be in a hurry to flip your food. This is because most foods undergo a chemical reaction called the Maillard reaction which creates a charred layer on the food by raising it to a certain temperature. This reaction is also responsible for what is commonly known as a "sear." Giving your food enough time to sear before flipping will ensure it does not stick.

Various Brands of Outdoor Griddle Grill

1. Blackstone Gas Type Griddle Grill Station

2. Blackstone Outdoor Flat Top Gas Type Grill Griddle Station

3. Camp Chef Flat Top

4. Blackstone Grill & Portable Gas Table Top Grill Griddle

5. Cuisinart Gas Grill Griddle Cooking Center

6. Blackstone Propane Gas Griddle Cooking Station

7. Presto 07061 Electric Grill Griddle

8. Royal Gourmet Event Gas Type Grill

9. Cuisinart GR-4N 5-In-1 Type Griddle

10. Barton Flat Top Griddle Type And Deep Fryer

11. Royal Gourmet Portable Propane Gas Type Grill And Griddle Combo

The Benefits of Griddle Grilling

Charcoal grilling has been the standard for many years, but it carries a whole host of risks. First of all, charcoal fires increase the risk of fires in your yard. That's pretty bad, but did you know that cooking with charcoal also increases your risk of cancer? The combination of charcoal, lighter fluid and dripping fats causes a variety of compounds that are considered carcinogenic. And you're not just breathing these chemicals when you cook. They're actually coating your food! Charcoal grills also contribute to air pollution by releasing large amounts of carbon monoxide and carbon dioxide into the atmosphere. The Blackstone Griddle, on the other hand, uses no charcoal and is much safer to use.

How to Clean and Store it?

After each use you will want to clean your griddle, but your griddle should not be cleaned like regular pots and pans. Since you want to build up a nice coating of seasoning to protect your griddle and get the best possible results, you need to make sure not to use things like dish soap to clean the cooking surface. Most detergents have a grease cutting ingredient and this will eat right through your layer of seasoning. The best way to clean your griddle is the way the pros do in restaurants: with a griddle scraper and hot water. You can purchase a griddle scraper which is designed to get rid of any bits of food left behind without sacrificing the seasoning layer you've achieved. To remove things like fat or sauces, a wash with very hot water will dissolve most things, which you can then scrape away. While you don't have to season your grill after every cleaning, continuous seasoning will ensure that your griddle stays dark and shiny.

Chapter 2: Tips and Tricks of Griddle Grilling

While cooking, food can be set in corners of the grill top to start warming or stay hot until serving.

Prep and chop ingredients ahead of time. Use ramekins or small bowls to measure out liquids and seasonings before cooking. Use zipper locking bags to hold food and marinades together and dump directly on the grill for easy cleanup. An old beer or soda six pack holder makes a great carrier for your oils, squirt bottles and seasonings.

Plastic squeeze bottles are great for holding oils and fresh water to clean your grill top with, as well as make it easy to squirt high proof alcohols like Bacardi 151, for your flambéed desserts.

Cleaning the Outdoor Griddle Cooktop

Once you receive your unique, handcrafted Backyard Hibachi, and periodically throughout the life of the grill, you will want to clean and season the grill top for enhanced cooking. The more you use and cook on your Backyard Hibachi, the better seasoned your grill top will become.

To Clean: Use dish soap and water to clean your grill and remove any dust when you receive it. Rinse well. Your grill is ready to go.

To season: Your Backyard Hibachi comes pre-seasoned and ready to cook on. However, if you would like to season it a little more, it is simple. Just heat your grill top, add some cooking oil and spread the oil carefully over the cooking surface. Allow the grill to heat and absorb oil for a few minutes, then get cooking!

Remember, like a good cast iron skillet, the more you cook on your hibachi, the better seasoned it will become.

Tools That Needed to Griddle Grilling

Cooking Utensils

2 spatulas & a scraper

Cheese Melting Cover

Useful for melting cheese on top of your creations, helping to speed cooking and also adding a little steam when needed.

Carry All Caddy

This handy carrier holds all your oils, sauces and seasonings for easy organization on your hibachi grill.

The Best Oils to Use

We always keep several different oils around the house for using in different recipes on the Backyard Hibachi grill. Many of the oils used in our recipes are suggestions, but you can substitute them for your favorites.

In the Asian cooking aisle at many grocery stores, you can find stir fry oils, which often have garlic and other flavors infused into the oil. These make great cooking oils and add extra flavor to already flavorful recipes.

Grapeseed oil is great high-heat cooking oil that has a light flavor that won't overpower your dish. Coconut oil cooks well on the hibachi at any heat and can add delicious, fresh flavor to any dish. Avocado oil is good high heat cooking oil. Toasted sesame oil is great for cooking with and to add toasty flavor to any dish.

Chapter 3: Common FAQs of Griddle Grilling

How do you Season the Cooking Surface?

Like most high quality cooking appliances, the cold rolled steel cooking surface of your Blackstone Griddle needs to be properly seasoned to ensure optimal cooking results. So you may be asking, **"what is seasoning?"** Before non-stick coatings existed, there was only one way to make sure food didn't stick to the cooking surface. By creating a layer of burnt on oil, you will not only achieve a perfect non-stick surface, you will also protect the cooking surface from scratches and oxidation. Let's get started.

First, use soap and water to thoroughly wash the cooking surface. Use a cloth to dry the surface. Next, apply a small amount of oil to the cooking surface. The best oils to use are those with a high smoke point like vegetable or canola.

Use a paper towel to spread the oil evenly across the cooking surface. Turn on all four burners and set the temperature to 275°F. Wait until the oil begins to smoke and the surface begins to darken.

Once it is smoking, turn off the burners and allows the griddle to cool. Repeat this process two to three more times until the entire surface is evenly dark. Now your griddle is naturally non-stick and protected from damage and rust.

How do you keep your Griddle Working from Season to Season?

Because you are most likely going to keep your griddle outside, you will need to make sure to do a few things before you store it and before you use it again after being stored. Before you store, make sure to disconnect the gas tank and store away from the griddle with a cap on the valve. You can also purchase a cover for the griddle to keep out insects and dust. When you are ready to start using your griddle again, make sure to check the burner area for spider webs. Webs are flammable and can cause flare ups if you do not clean them out before cooking. Check the level in your gas tank to make sure you have enough fuel to start cooking. Once the tank is attached and you are ready to cook, it's a good idea to perform a new season on the cooking surface. Simply follow the instructions above and your griddle will be good as new.

Chapter 4: Breakfasts and Brunches

Fried Pickles

Prep. Time: 10 minutes / Cook Time: 10 minutes / Serves: 4

Ingredients:

- 20 dill pickle slices
- 1/4 cup all-purpose flour
- 1/8 tsp. baking powder
- 3 tbsps. beer or seltzer water
- 1/8 tsp. sea salt
- 2 tbsps. water, plus more if needed
- 2 tbsps. cornstarch
- 1-1/2 cups panko bread crumbs
- 1 tsp. paprika
- 1 tsp. garlic powder
- 1/4 tsp. cayenne pepper
- 2 tbsps. canola oil, divided

Directions:

1. Preheat the griddle to medium-high.
2. Pat the pickle slices dry, and place them on a dry plate in the freezer.
3. In a medium bowl, stir together the flour, baking powder, beer, salt, and water. The batter should be the consistency of cake batter. If it is too thick, add more water, 1 teaspoon at a time.
4. Place the cornstarch in a small shallow bowl.
5. In a separate large shallow bowl, combine the bread crumbs, paprika, garlic powder, and cayenne pepper.

6. Remove the pickles from the freezer. Dredge each one in cornstarch. Tap off any excess, then coat in the batter. Lastly, coat evenly with the bread crumb mixture.
7. Set on the griddle top and gently brush the breaded pickles with 1 tablespoon of oil. Cook for 5 minutes.
8. After 5 minutes, turn and gently brush the pickles with the remaining 1 tablespoon of oil and resume cooking.
9. When cooking is complete, serve immediately.

Nutrition value per serving:

Calories: 296kcal; Fat: 10g; Carbs: 44g; Protein: 7g

Grilled Fruit Salad with Honey-Lime Glaze

Prep. Time: 10 minutes / Cook Time: 4 minutes / Serves: 4

Ingredients:

- 1/2 pound strawberries, washed, hulled and halved
- 1 (9 oz.) can pineapple chunks, drained, juice reserved
- 2 peaches, pitted and sliced
- 6 tbsps. honey, divided
- 1 tbsp. freshly squeezed lime juice

Directions:

1. Preheat your griddle to medium high.
2. While the unit is preheating, combine the strawberries, pineapple, and peaches in a large bowl with 3 tablespoons of honey. Toss to coat evenly.
3. Place the fruit on the grill top. Gently press the fruit down to maximize grill marks. Grill for 4 minutes without flipping.
4. Meanwhile, in a small bowl, combine the remaining 3 tablespoons of honey, lime juice, and 1 tablespoon of reserved pineapple juice.
5. When cooking is complete, place the fruit in a large bowl and toss with the honey mixture. Serve immediately.

Nutrition value per serving:

Calories: 178kcal; fat: 1g; Carbs: 47g; Protein: 2g

Onion, Pepper, and Mushroom Frittata

Prep. Time: 10 minutes / Cook Time: 10 minutes / Serves: 4 slices

Ingredients:

- 4 large eggs
- 1/4 cup whole milk
- Sea salt
- Freshly ground black pepper
- 1/2 bell pepper, seeded and diced
- 1/2 onion, chopped
- 4 cremini mushrooms, sliced
- 1/2 cup shredded Cheddar cheese

Directions:

1. Preheat the griddle to medium high.
2. In a medium bowl, whisk together the eggs and milk. Season with the salt and pepper. Add the bell pepper, onion, mushrooms, and cheese. Mix until well combined.
3. Pour the egg mixture into the Ninja Multi-Purpose Pan or baking pan, spreading evenly.
4. Place the pan directly to the grill and cook for 10 minutes, or until lightly golden.

Nutrition value per serving:

Calories: 153kcal; Fat: 10g; Carbs: 5g; Protein: 11g

Classic Buttermilk Pancakes

Prep time: 5 minutes/ Cook time: 10 minutes / Serves: 4

Ingredients:

- 2 cup all-purpose flour
- 3 tbsps. sugar
- 1-1/2 tsps. baking powder
- 1-1/2 tsps. baking soda
- 1-1/4 tsps. salt
- 2-1/2 cup buttermilk
- 2 eggs
- 3 tbsps. unsalted butter, melted
- 2 tbsps. vegetable oil

Directions:

1. In a large bowl, combine the flour, sugar, baking soda, baking powder, and salt.
2. Stir in the buttermilk, eggs, and butter, and mix until combined but not totally smooth.
3. Heat your griddle to medium heat and add a small amount of oil. Using a paper towel, spread the oil over the griddle in a very thin layer.
4. Use a ladle to pour the batter onto the griddle allowing a few inches between pancakes.
5. When the surface of the pancakes is bubbly, flip and cook a few additional minutes. Remove the pancakes from the griddle and serve immediately with butter and maple syrup.

Nutrition value per serving:

Calories: 432kcal, Fat: 12.8.g, Carbs: 65.1g, Protein: 14.4g

Fluffy Blueberry Pancakes

Prep time: 10 minutes /Cook time: 10 minutes /Serves: 2

Ingredients:

- 1 cup flour
- 3/4 cup milk
- 2 tbsps. white vinegar
- 2 tbsps. sugar
- 1 tsp. baking powder
- 1/2 tsp. baking soda
- 1/2 tsp. salt
- 1 egg
- 2 tbsps. butter, melted
- 1cup fresh blueberries
- butter for cooking

Directions:

1. In a bowl, combine the milk and vinegar. Set aside for two minutes.
2. In a large bowl, combine the flour, sugar, baking powder, baking soda, and salt. Stir in the milk, egg, blueberries, and melted butter. Mix until combined but not totally smooth.
3. Heat your griddle to medium heat and add a little butter. Pour the pancakes onto the griddle and cook until one side is golden brown. Flip the pancakes and cook until the other side is golden.
4. Remove the pancakes from the griddle and serve with warm maple syrup.

Nutrition value per serving:

Calories: 499kcal, Fat: 16.5.g, Carbs: 76.2g, Protein: 12.9g

Baked Egg and Bacon–Stuffed Peppers

Prep. Time: 10 minutes / Cook Time: 15 minutes / Serves: 4 slices

Ingredients:

- 1 cup shredded Cheddar cheese
- 4 slices bacon, cooked and chopped
- 4 bell peppers, seeded and tops removed
- 4 large eggs
- Sea salt
- Freshly ground black pepper
- Chopped fresh parsley, for garnish

Directions:

1. Preheat the griddle to medium high.
2. Divide the cheese and bacon between the bell peppers. Crack one of the eggs into each bell pepper, and season with salt and pepper.
3. Place each bell pepper to the grill and cook for 10 to 15 minutes, until the egg whites are cooked and the yolks are slightly runny.
4. Remove the peppers, garnish with parsley, and serve.

Nutrition value per serving:

Calories: 326kcal; Fat: 23g; Carbs: 10g; Protein: 22g

Grilled Pizza with Eggs and Greens

Prep. Time: 10 minutes / Cook Time: 8 minutes / Serves: 2 slices

Ingredients:

- 2 tbsps. all-purpose flour, plus more as needed
- 1/2 store-bought pizza dough (about 8 ounces)
- 1 tbsp. canola oil, divided
- 1 cup fresh ricotta cheese
- 4 large eggs
- Sea salt
- Freshly ground black pepper
- 4 cups arugula, torn
- 1 tbsp. extra-virgin olive oil
- 1 tsp. freshly squeezed lemon juice
- 2 tbsps. grated Parmesan cheese

Directions:

1. Preheat the griddle to medium high.
2. Dust a clean work surface with flour. Place the dough on the floured surface, and roll it into a 9-inch round of even thickness. Dust your rolling pin and work surface with additional flour, as needed, to ensure the dough does not stick.
3. Brush the surface of the rolled-out dough evenly with 1/2 tablespoon of canola oil. Flip the dough over and brush with the remaining 1/2 tablespoon oil. Poke the dough with a fork 5 or 6 times across its surface to prevent air pockets from forming during cooking.
4. Place the dough to the grill and cook for 4 minutes.
5. After 4 minutes, flip the dough, then spoon teaspoons of ricotta cheese across the surface of the dough, leaving a 1-inch border around the edges.
6. Crack one egg into a ramekin or small bowl. This way you can easily remove any shell that may break into the egg and keep the yolk intact.

25

Imagine the dough is split into four quadrants. Pour one egg into each. Repeat with the remaining 3 eggs. Season the pizza with salt and pepper.

7. Continue cooking for the remaining 3 to 4 minutes, until the egg whites are firm.
8. Meanwhile, in a medium bowl, toss together the arugula, oil, and lemon juice, and season with salt and pepper.
9. Transfer the pizza to a cutting board and let it cool. Top it with the arugula mixture, drizzle with olive oil, if desired, and sprinkle with Parmesan cheese. Cut into pieces and serve.

Nutrition value per serving:

Calories: 788kcal; Fat: 46g; Carbs: 58g; Protein: 34g

Sausage Mixed Grill

Prep. Time: 5 minutes / Cook Time: 22 minutes / Serves: 4 slices

Ingredients:

- 8 mini bell peppers
- 2 heads radicchio, each cut into 6 wedges
- Canola oil, for brushing
- Sea salt
- Freshly ground black pepper
- 6 breakfast sausage links
- 6 hot or sweet Italian sausage links

Directions:

1. Preheat the griddle to medium high.
2. Brush the bell peppers and radicchio with the oil. Season with salt and black pepper.
3. Place the bell peppers and radicchio on the Grill and cook for 10 minutes, without flipping.
4. Meanwhile, poke the sausages with a fork or knife and brush them with some of the oil.
5. After 10 minutes, remove the vegetables and set aside. Decrease the heat to medium. Place the sausages on the Grill and cook for 6 minutes.
6. Flip the sausages and cook for 6 minutes more. Remove the sausages from the Grill.
7. Serve the sausages and vegetables on a large cutting board or serving tray.

Nutrition value per serving:

Calories: 473kcal; Fat: 34g; Carbs: 14g; Protein: 28g

Bacon and Gruyere Omelet

Prep Time: 5 minutes / Cook Time: 15 minutes / Serves: 2

Ingredients:

- 6 eggs, beaten
- 6 strips bacon
- 1/4 pound gruyere, shredded
- 1 tsp. black pepper
- 1 tsp. salt
- 1 tbsp. chives, finely chopped
- vegetable oil

Directions:

1. Add salt to the beaten eggs and set aside for 10 minutes.
2. Heat your griddle to medium heat and add the bacon strips. Cook until most of the fat has rendered, but bacon is still flexible. Remove the bacon from the griddle and place on paper towels.
3. Once the bacon has drained, chop into small pieces.
4. Add the eggs to the griddle in two even pools. Cook until the bottom of the eggs starts to firm up. Add the gruyere to the eggs and cook until the cheese has started to melt and the eggs are just starting to brown.
5. Add the bacon pieces and use a spatula to turn one half of the omelet onto the other half. Remove from the griddle, season with pepper and chives and serve.

Nutrition value per serving:

Calories: 734kcal, Fat: 55.3.g, Carbs: 2.8g, Protein: 54.8g

Grilled Cinnamon Toast with Berries and Whipped Cream

Prep. Time: 15 minutes / Cook Time: 10 minutes / Serves: 4 slices

Ingredients:

- 1 (15-ounce) can full-fat coconut milk, refrigerated overnight
- 1/2 tablespoon powdered sugar
- 1-1/2 teaspoons vanilla extract, divided
- 1 cup halved strawberries
- 1 tablespoon maple syrup, plus more for garnish
- 1 tablespoon brown sugar, divided
- 3/4 cup lite coconut milk
- 2 large eggs
- 1/2 teaspoon ground cinnamon
- 2 tablespoons unsalted butter, at room temperature
- 4 slices challah bread

Directions:

1. Turn the chilled can of full-fat coconut milk upside down (do not shake the can), open the bottom, and pour out the liquid coconut water. Scoop the remaining solid coconut cream into a medium bowl. Using an electric hand mixer, whip the cream for 3 to 5 minutes, until soft peaks form.
2. Add the powdered sugar and 1/2 teaspoon of the vanilla to the coconut cream, and whip it again until creamy. Place the bowl in the refrigerator.
3. Preheat the griddle to medium high.
4. While the unit is preheating, combine the strawberries with the maple syrup and toss to coat evenly. Sprinkle evenly with ½ tablespoon of the brown sugar.

5. In a large shallow bowl, whisk together the lite coconut milk, eggs, the remaining 1 teaspoon of vanilla, and cinnamon.
6. Place the strawberries on the grill top. Gently press the fruit down to maximize grill marks. Grill for 4 minutes without flipping.
7. Meanwhile, butter each slice of bread on both sides. Place one slice in the egg mixture and let it soak for 1 minute. Flip the slice over and soak it for another minute. Repeat with the remaining bread slices. Sprinkle each side of the toast with the remaining 1/2 tablespoon of brown sugar.
8. After 4 minutes, remove the strawberries from the grill and set aside. Decrease the temperature to medium low. Place the bread on the Grill and cook for 4 to 6 minutes, until golden and caramelized. Check often to ensure desired doneness.
9. Place the toast on a plate and top with the strawberries and whipped coconut cream. Drizzle with maple syrup, if desired.

Nutrition value per serving:

Calories: 386kcal; Fat: 19g; Carbs: 49g; Protein: 7g

Lemon-Garlic Artichokes

Prep. Time: 10 minutes / Cook Time: 15 minutes / Serves: 4 slices

Ingredients:

- Juice of 1/2 lemon
- 1/2 cup canola oil
- 3 garlic cloves, chopped
- Sea salt
- Freshly ground black pepper
- 2 large artichokes, trimmed and halved

Directions:

1. Preheat the griddle to medium high.
2. While the unit is preheating, in a medium bowl, combine the lemon juice, oil, and garlic. Season with salt and pepper, then brush the artichoke halves with the lemon-garlic mixture.
3. Place the artichokes on the Grill, cut side down. Gently press them down to maximize grill marks. Grill for 8 to 10 minutes, occasionally basting generously with the lemon-garlic mixture throughout cooking, until blistered on all sides.

Nutrition value per serving:

Calories: 285kcal; Fat: 28g; Carbs: 10g; Protein: 3g

Blistered Green Beans

Prep. Time: 5 minutes / Cook Time: 10 minutes / Serves: 4 slices

Ingredients:

- 1 pound haricots verts or green beans, trimmed
- 2 tablespoons vegetable oil
- Juice of 1 lemon
- Pinch red pepper flakes
- Flaky sea salt
- Freshly ground black pepper

Directions:

1. Preheat the griddle to medium high.
2. While the unit is preheating, in a medium bowl, toss the green beans in oil until evenly coated.
3. Place the green beans on the Grill and grill for 8 to 10 minutes, tossing frequently until blistered on all sides.
4. When cooking is complete, place the green beans on a large serving platter. Squeeze lemon juice over the green beans, top with red pepper flakes, and season with sea salt and black pepper.

Nutrition value per serving:

Calories: 100kcal; Fat: 7g; Carbs: 10g; Protein: 2g

Grilled Asian-Style Broccoli

Prep. Time: 10 minutes / Cook Time: 10 minutes / Serves: 4 slices

Ingredients:

- 4 tablespoons soy sauce
- 4 tablespoons balsamic vinegar
- 2 tablespoons canola oil
- 2 teaspoons maple syrup
- 2 heads broccoli, trimmed into florets
- Red pepper flakes, for garnish
- Sesame seeds, for garnish

Directions:

1. Preheat the griddle to medium high.
2. While the unit is preheating, in a large bowl, whisk together the soy sauce, balsamic vinegar, oil, and maple syrup. Add the broccoli and toss to coat evenly.
3. Place the broccoli on the Grill and grill for 8 to 10 minutes, until charred on all sides.
4. When cooking is complete, place the broccoli on a large serving platter. Garnish with red pepper flakes and sesame seeds. Serve immediately.

Nutrition value per serving:

Calories: 133kcal; Fat: 8g; Carbs: 13g; Protein: 5g

Chapter 5: Dinners

Lemon Pepper Marinated Pork

Prep. Time: 5 minutes / Cook Time: 10 minutes / Serves: 4 slices

Ingredients:

- Red onion sliced into rings
- Juice of 1 lemon
- 1 tsp. ground black pepper
- 1/2 tsp. chili powder
- 1/4 cup soy sauce
- 2 cloves garlic chopped
- 1 tbsp. coconut sugar (or use 1 tsp. honey)
- 1 lb. sukiyaki cut lean pork (any tender part)
- 1 tbsp. oil for frying
- Green onion for garnish

Directions:

1. In a bowl, combine the pork, soy sauce, lemon juice, chili powder, black pepper, coconut sugar, and garlic.
2. Mix everything together and let stand for 30 minutes in room temperature or up to overnight in the fridge.
3. Preheat griddle to medium heat and prepare with oil
4. Add the pork to your flat top. Cook both sides for about 2 minutes each, spoon the marinade or pork and cook until marinade dries up.
5. Add the red onion rings and sauté for about 2 more minutes.
6. Transfer to a serving dish.
7. Top with chopped green onions and serve with rice or just lettuce. Serves 2-4

Nutrition value per serving:

Calories: 379kcal; fat: 12g; Carbs: 2.1g; Protein: 40.7 g

Honey Paprika Chicken Tenders Recipe

Prep. Time: 5 minutes / Cook Time: 10 minutes / Serves: 4 slices

Ingredients:

- 1 lb. chicken tenders, sliced into finger-thick slices
- 1/2 cup honey
- 1/3 cup dark soy sauce
- 3 tbsps. olive oil
- 1 tbsp. paprika
- 2 tbsps. curry powder
- Salt and pepper to taste

Directions:

1. Preheat your griddle to medium-high.
2. Slice the chicken into half an inch-thick strips so they will cook faster and absorb more flavor.
3. In a bowl, combine the soy sauce, paprika, curry powder, honey, and olive oil.
4. Dump in the chicken and mix. Season with salt and pepper to taste.
5. Let the mixture stand for 10-15 minutes.
6. Place on griddle to cook half-way through.
7. Remove from flat top and transfer to a roasting pan and spread evenly so that the chicken pieces are just 1 layer.
8. Cover with aluminum foil and place roasting pan back on flat top until fully cooked through. Approximately 10 – 12 minutes.
9. Garnish with spring onion and enjoy!

Nutrition value per serving:

Calories: 619kcal, fat: 13g; Carbs: 39g; Protein: 4g

Sizzling Chicken Mushroom Recipe

Prep. Time: 10 minutes / Cook Time: 15 minutes / Serves: 4 slices

Ingredients:

- 1/2 lb. chicken breast, cut into strips
- 1/2 cup button mushrooms, sliced
- 1/2 cup frozen green peas, thawed
- 1/2 cup water
- 1 tbsp. soy sauce
- A pinch ground black pepper
- 1 tsp. cornstarch
- 1 tsp. onion powder

Directions:

1. Make sure you got all of your ingredients ready to go.
2. Prepare your griddle to medium-high and place the chicken on it until cooked.
3. Add the mushrooms and the peas and cook for 3 minutes.
4. To make the sauce or the gravy, mix together the water, soy sauce, ground pepper, onion powder and cornstarch.
5. Place aluminum roasting pan on your flat top. Combine the chicken, mushrooms and peas mixture in roasting pan. It will thicken immediately. Stir for another 3 to 5 minutes. Take off the heat and serve.
6. The dish easily serves two persons and the recipe can be easily doubled to feed more. Enjoy!

Nutrition value per serving:

Calories: 206kcal | Carbs: 2g | Protein: 23g | Fat: 11g

Southern Fried Turkey Strips with Stuffed Mushrooms

Prep. Time: 10 minutes / Cook Time: 15 minutes / Serves: 4 slices

Ingredients:

- 4 * 4 oz. turkey steaks
- 4 large portabella mushrooms
- 1/3 cup extra virgin olive oil
- 2 tbsps. tomato paste
- 1/2 c. almonds
- 1 tsp. black pepper
- 1 tsp. cayenne pepper
- 1 tsp. paprika powder
- 1 tsp. salt
- 1/2 cup shredded cheddar cheese

Directions:

1. Place the almonds, black pepper, cayenne pepper, paprika powder and salt into the food processor and blend until the almonds become fully powdered.
2. Once the almonds and other ingredients have become fully powdered, add them to the mixing bowl along with the extra virgin olive oil, then mix them together with the wooden spoon to form a marinade.
3. Once the marinade ingredients are fully mixed, add the turkey steaks to the mixing bowl and coat them fully in the marinade.
   Once the turkey steaks are fully coated in marinade, pour them into the sealable container and put the container into the refrigerator for a minimum of 4 hours to allow the marinade to fully soak into the turkey steaks. If you have time, turn the turkey steaks halfway through to ensure that the marinade soaks into them evenly.
4. Prepare griddle for medium heat. Lightly oil. Place on chicken on griddle. Cover with basting cover. Add a little water to the surface before you cover. Until cooked through.

5. Spread an equal amount of tomato paste on the base of each portabella mushroom and then top with an equal amount of shredded cheddar cheese. Place on griddle, cover until cheese is melted.
6. Place one southern fried turkey steak and one stuffed portabella mushroom onto each of the four plates, serve and enjoy.

Nutrition value per serving:

calories 175.9kcal; fat 3g; protein 5.3 g; carbohydrates 2.9 g

Orange-Cranberry Bone-In Chicken Breasts

Prep. Time: 5 minutes / Cook Time: 15 minutes / Serves: 4 slices

Ingredients:

- 2 tbsps. coconut oil
- 2 lbs. bone-in chicken breasts, with skin
- 1-1/2 tsps. fresh sage, chopped
- 1-1/2 tsps. fresh thyme leaves
- Sea salt and black pepper, to taste
- 1/2 cup fresh (or frozen) cranberries
- 2 tbsps. freshly squeezed orange juice
- 2 tbsps. honey, preferably local
- 1/4 tsp. ground cinnamon
- 1/2 tsp. ground ginger
- 1/4 tsp. ground cloves
- 1/8 tsp. ground nutmeg

Directions:

1. Melt the coconut oil in a large, aluminum roasting pan over medium heat. Season the chicken with sage, and thyme. Season with salt and black pepper, to taste.
2. Prepare griddle for medium heat. Lightly oil. Place seasoned chicken in griddle skin-side down and cook until browned, approximately 4-5 minutes, or until it releases easily from the bottom of the pan. Turn the chicken and continue cooking another 4-5 minutes on the remaining side.
3. While the chicken is browning, add the cranberries, orange juice, honey, cinnamon, ginger, cloves, and nutmeg to aluminum roasting pan. Place over medium heat and bring it to a gentle boil. Cook until the cranberries pop open and the sauce becomes slightly thickened, around 4-5 minutes.

4. Place chicken in roasting pan on your flat top. Cover and "roast" until the chicken is fully cooked through and the sauce is bubbly, around 15 to 20 minutes or until chicken is cooked through and reaches an internal temperature of 160°F.*
5. Remove from pan and transfer chicken to a serving platter. Cover loosely and let rest for 5 minutes before serving topped with the warm orange-cranberry pan sauce and your choice of sides. Enjoy!
6. *Internal temperature will continue to rise to 165°F as it rests.

Nutrition value per serving:

Calories 378kcal, Fat 3.1g, Protein 40.1g, Carbs 46.5g

Steak

Prep. Time: 5 minutes / Cook Time: 10 minutes / Serves: 4-5 slices

Ingredients:

- 1 steak
- 1 salt
- 1 pepper

Directions:

1. This recipe is for any number of steaks including sirloin, T-bone, ribeye, etc.
2. Season your steak with salt and pepper, or any other seasoning of your choice.
3. Prepare griddle for medium-high heat. Lightly oil. Place steak on griddle.
4. When one side develops a crust, flip once. Until the steak is done to your desired doneness.
5. The most important point to remember when griddling a steak is to leave it alone. Let the juices, the seasoning and the heat make an excellent steak.

Nutrition value per serving:

Calories: 919kcal, Carbs: 4g, Protein: 61g, Fat: 73g

Herb-Rubbed, Bone-In Pork Chops

Prep. Time: 5 minutes / Cook Time: 5 minutes / Serves: 4 slices

Ingredients:

- 2 tbsps. Kosher salt
- 8 large fresh basil leaves, torn into pieces
- 2 stems fresh rosemary, leaves stripped from stems and crushed
- 2 tbsps. fresh thyme leaves, crushed with fingers
- 3 cloves garlic, smashed, peeled and roughly chopped
- 1 tbsps. salt
- 4 thick-cut bone-in pork chops, approximately 1" thick

Directions:

1. Combine salt, basil, rosemary, thyme, garlic and pepper thoroughly in a small bowl. Rub mixture over all sides of pork chops until thoroughly covered.
2. Prepare griddle for medium heat. Lightly oil. Place on griddle. Cook for 7-8 minutes, turn once. Cover with basting cover. Add a little water to the surface before you cover. If your chops are thinner or thicker than 1", adjust cook time accordingly.
3. Remove chops from heat, cover and let rest for 3 - 5 minutes before serving. Serve with a summer vegetable medley and top with a pat of compound butter seasoned with the same herbs used in the rub.

Nutrition value per serving:

calories 221kcal, fat 11g, carbs 1g, protein 26g

Maple-Balsamic Boneless Pork Chops

Prep. Time: 10 minutes / Cook Time: 10 minutes / Serves: 4 slices

Ingredients:

- 1 tbsp. extra virgin olive oil
- 4 (4-oz.) boneless pork chops
- Salt and black pepper, to taste
- 1/2 cup balsamic vinegar
- 2-1/2 tbsps. real maple syrup

Directions:

1. Prepare griddle for medium heat. Lightly oil.
2. Season pork chops on each side with salt and pepper, to taste, and add to the pre-heated griddle. Brown pork chops on each side, approximately 3 minutes per side. Remove pork chops from pan and set aside on a rimmed dish.
3. Place small aluminum roasting pan to your flat top. Heat this heat zone to high. Add balsamic vinegar and maple syrup and bring to a boil, stirring constantly.
4. Reduce heat to medium and cook mixture until it is reduced to about 1/3 of its original volume. When ready, the glaze will become thick and syrupy. (Do not overcook or the mixture will become hard and sticky).
5. Transfer chops to a serving platter or individual serving plate and drizzle with pan sauce. Serve immediately with griddled Brussels sprouts or your choice of sides.

Nutrition value per serving:

Calories 351.2kcal; protein 25.7 g; carbs 33.2 g; fat 20g

Beef Honey Curry Stir Fry Recipe

Prep. Time: 5 minutes / Cook Time: 10 minutes / Serves: 3-4 slices

Ingredients:

- 1/2 lb. sukiyaki cut beef
- 1/2 cup honey
- 1/2 cup soy sauce
- 4 tbsps. curry powder
- 4 tbsps. oil
- 1 tsp. ground black pepper
- 1 medium sized red onion, sliced
- 1 medium sized red bell pepper, sliced into strips
- 1 medium sized green bell pepper, sliced into strips
- 1 medium sized yellow bell pepper, sliced into strips
- Roasting pan

Directions:

1. Prepare all the ingredients that you'll need.
2. Marinate the beef with marinade made of soy sauce, curry powder, honey and ground black pepper and let it stand for 15 minutes.
3. Prepare your flat top to medium high heat. Oil and sauté the red bell pepper, green bell pepper, red onion and yellow bell pepper for a few minutes (usually just a little over a minute), taking care that the vegetables are cooked but not wilted. They should remain crunchy for great texture. Take the cooked vegetables off the pan and set aside.
4. Remove beef from marinate mixed and place on griddle until halfway cooked. Remove and place in roasting pan.
5. Place roasting pan on griddle and add in the remaining half of the oil and marinade and cook the beef together with the marinade over medium heat until the sauce thickens, and the beef is cooked through. This only takes 5-7 minutes. Turn off the heat.

6. Toss the cooked vegetables with the beef in the pain to coat it with some of the sauce and bring all flavors together. Serve over steaming hot rice, mashed potato, or even pasta! This recipe makes for about 3-4 servings.

Nutrition value per serving:

Calories: 473.68kcal Carbs: 16.02g Protein: 24.21g Fat: 34.34g

Smoked Pork Sausage Hakka Noodles Recipe

Prep. Time: 5 minutes / Cook Time: 15 minutes / Serves: 4 slices

Ingredients:

- 1 packet Hakka Noodles
- 5 Smoked Pork Sausages
- 50g Coriander Leaves
- 1 tbsp. Soya Sauce
- 50g Mint Leaves
- 1 Onion
- 3 Green Chilies
- 1 Capsicum
- Salt to Taste

Directions:

1. Cut and slice all the pork vegetables and keep it aside.
2. Then cook the packet of Hakka noodle in a container. Make sure to add a little bit of oil so that they don't stick together. Boil the noodles for 5-6 minutes.
3. Take the noodles and transfer them to a strainer and wash them under the tap so that they stop cooking.
4. Then add a little bit of oil and soya sauce to the noodles. Once this is ready, we are ready to cook the rest of the meal.
5. Prepare griddle for medium heat. Lightly oil. Add the onions and chilies till they turn light brown.
6. Then add the smoked pork sausages and cook it for 5 – 7 minutes.
7. Add the coriander and mint leaves and cook for another 5 minutes. The major aroma will be from the coriander and mint leaves.
8. Then add the cauliflower, capsicum and salt to taste.
9. Then add the noodles and then cook it for another 5 minutes.
10. Take it off the griddle and then serve it with mint leaves.

Nutrition value per serving:

Calories 220.2kcal; protein 25.7 g; carbs 33.2 g; fat 23g

Asian Style Beef Broccoli Recipe

Prep. Time: 5 minutes / Cook Time: 10 minutes / Serves: 2-4 slices

Ingredients:

- 1/2 lb. sukiyaki cut beef (very thin across the grain slices)
- 3 cups Chinese broccoli
- 1/3 cup brown sugar
- 1/3 cup water
- 1/3 cup soy sauce
- 3 tbsps. cooking oil
- 2 tbsps. browned chopped garlic (you may use garlic flakes)
- 2 tbsps. sesame oil
- 1/2 tsp. red chili flakes
- 1/2 tsp. freshly grounded black pepper

Directions:

1. Get all of your ingredients together.
2. Prepare griddle for medium heat. Lightly oil. Place on broccoli on flat top. Cover with basting cover. Add a little water to the surface before you cover to steam Chinese broccoli until it is done but not soggy. It is important to retain the bright green color for the visual appeal of the meal; plus the crunchy texture of the cooked vegetable add a certain freshness to the dish.
3. Cook the beef in the cooking oil until browned. It would only take 3 minutes in medium to high heat because the beef is very thinly cut.
4. Once the beef has been cooked and browned, add in the water, soy sauce, brown sugar, half of the garlic, the red chili flakes and black pepper. Simmer for 3 minutes.
5. On a serving dish, arrange the Chinese broccoli and spoon the cooked beef and the sauce over it. Top with the rest of the garlic flakes and drizzle in the sesame oil.

6. Serve and enjoy! This recipe serves 2-4 individuals depending if the dish is to be served as a side dish or a main dish. It's a visual treat for sure!

Nutrition value per serving:

calories 331.4kcal; protein 21.7 g; carbs 13.3 g; fat 15g.

Chapter 6: Red Meat Recipes

Griddle Baked Beef Stew

Prep. Time: 15 minutes / Cook Time: 5 hours / Serves: 8

Ingredients:

- 2-1/2 lbs. beef stew meat chunks
- 8 carrots, chopped
- 3 medium white onions, quartered
- 5 medium white potatoes, quartered
- 2 cans Sweet Peas
- 2 bay leaves
- 2 beef bouillon cubes
- 1 tbsp. sugar
- 1 tbsp. salt
- 1/4 tbsp. thyme
- 1 tbsp. black pepper
- 1/4 cup cornstarch
- 1 (28-oz.) can whole tomatoes
- 1 cup water

Directions:

1. Preheat the griddle to medium high.
2. Pour all the ingredients in a Skillet and set on the griddle.
3. Cover and cook for 5 hours, stir once or twice
4. Serve immediately and enjoy.

Nutrition value per serving:

calories 439kcal, fat 13g, carbs50g, protein30g

Lumberjack Steak and Potatoes

Prep. Time: 20 minutes / Cook Time: 22 Minutes / Serves: 4

Ingredients:

- 1 lb. Boneless beef sirloin steak, cut into 4 serving pieces
- 3/4 tsp. Seasoned salt
- 1/2 tsp. Garlic-pepper blend
- 1-1/2 cups frozen stir-fry vegetables
- 1 bag refrigerated home-style potato slices
- 4 oz. or 1/2 cup shredded American-cheddar cheese blend

Directions:

1. Preheat Griddle Grill to Sear with the unit closed.
2. Place the steak onto a griddle and sprinkle with the seasoned salt and garlic pepper.
3. Cook on medium heat for 3 minutes on each side.
4. Remove steak from griddle and add vegetables, cooking for 3 minutes.
5. Pour in potatoes and cook for 10 minutes.
6. When done, pour in the steak and mix together before serving.

Nutrition value per serving:

Calories 700.2kcal, fat 40g, Carbs 51.8 g, Protein70.1 g

Succulent Griddle-Seared Garlic Tenderloin

Prep. Time: 20 minutes / Cook Time: 8 minutes / Serves: 2

Ingredients:

- 12 oz. steaks (can use 2 6oz. flat iron tenderloin)
- 1 tbsp. Olive oil
- 1/2 teaspoon garlic powder
- 1/2 teaspoon onion powder
- 1/2 teaspoon black pepper
- 1 pinch of salt (to taste)

Directions:

1. Preheat Griddle Grill to Medium-High with the unit closed.
2. After bringing steak to room temperature, pat the meat with a paper towel to remove moisture. Season with the salt, pepper, onion and garlic powders.
3. Add oil to your griddle.
4. Let the steaks cook for a few minutes turning them over and repeating after first side is cooked, then flip and cook for another 3 minutes. Turn over the steaks and cook for another 2 to 3 minutes. Check steaks to see if they are cooked to your liking, but each side should be at least brown in color.
5. Slice and serve the steak after letting it cool for several minutes.

Nutrition value per serving:

Calories 667kcal; protein47 g; carbs18g; fat 20g

Thick Stacked Sizzling Burgers On The Griddle

Prep. Time: 20 Minutes / Cook Time: 8 minutes / Serves: 6

Ingredients:

- 1-1/2 pounds ground beef, 80% to 85% lean
- 6 hamburger buns
- 1/4 stick butter (use oil as substitute if desired)
- Pinch salt
- Pinch fresh black pepper
- 6 slices cheese

Burger toppings:

- 2 sliced tomatoes,
- 1/4 onion (sliced)
- 2 pickles
- 3 tbsp. Ketchup
- 2 tbsp. Mustard
- 6 lettuce leaves

Directions:

1. Preheat Griddle Grill to Sear with the unit closed.
2. Shape ground beef into 6 big and chunky patties, then melt butter on griddle over medium heat. Lightly butter the buns, then toasting them to your desired liking. Move the buns to a clean plate. Then, using the same pan, cook the patties for several minutes. Add a pinch of salt and pepper to each and continue to cook for 3 to 4 min.
3. Flip the burgers and repeat the process, adding a little more salt and pepper than before. Cook for another several minutes or until cooked to your desired liking.

Nutrition value per serving:

calories 980; fats 43g; Carbs 13.3 g; protein 9g

Pork Loin Roast

Prep. Time: 12 hours / Cook Time: 45 minutes / Serves: 4

Ingredients:

- 1 (3 lbs.) Pork Top Loin Roast
- Kosher Salt
- Black Pepper To Taste
- Orange Marmalade

Directions:

1. Remove any silver skin and excess fat from the loin. Trim the loin to be even in thickness throughout.
2. Coat the loin with Kosher salt liberally, place in a resealable bag, and refrigerate for at least 3 hours or overnight. This will dry brine the roast and keep it moist while it cooks.
3. Rinse the excess salt off the roast, pat it dry, and season it with black pepper.
4. Turn the Griddle grill on to high, and spray it with spray oil.
5. Cook the loin on high for several minutes per side until it pulls cleanly from the grill.
6. Remove the loin from the grill and allow it to relax for several minutes to allow the juices to redistribute.
7. Turn the grill down to medium, and return the loin to the grill. Cook for about 30 minutes, turning occasionally, until the internal temperature reaches 145 degrees.
8. Glaze the outside of the loin with the marmalade, and let it relax for at least 10 minutes before slicing and serving.

Nutrition value per serving:

calories 163; fats 7.5g; carbs 48g; Protein 19g

Pork Baby Back Ribs

Prep. Time: 15 minutes / Cook Time: 2 hours / Serves: 4

Ingredients:

- 2 lbs. baby back ribs
- olive oil
- salt and pepper to taste
- BBQ sauce

Directions:

1. Remove the membrane from the bone side of the ribs. Coat with olive oil and sprinkle with salt and pepper. Let stand for 10 minutes.
2. Heat up the griddle grill to medium, and place the ribs bone side to the heat. Cook for 1.5 hours or until the temperature is 190–195 degrees.
3. Remove the ribs from the grill and let them relax for 30 minutes.
4. Brush the ribs with BBQ sauce, and place on a hot grill for 2–3 minutes to set the sauce before serving.

Nutrition value per serving:

calories 290; fats 20g; carbohydrates 5g; Protein 23g

Pork Tenderloin

Prep. Time: 5 minutes / Cook Time: 25 minutes / Serves: 6

Ingredients:

- pork tenderloin
- olive oil
- salt and pepper to taste

Directions:

1. Remove the silver skin and fat from the pork tenderloin and trim to a similar thickness.
2. Brush with olive oil and sprinkle with salt and pepper.
3. Heat up the griddle grill to high, and cook for 3–4 minutes per side or until the meat removes easily from the grill.
4. Remove the tenderloins from the grill and let them relax for several minutes.
5. Turn the griddle grill to medium and return the tenderloins to the grill. Cook for 15–20 minutes or until the temperature is 145 degrees.
6. Remove the tenderloins from the grill, and let them relax for several minutes before serving.

Nutrition value per serving:

Calories: 122, Fat: 3g, Carbs: 8g, Protein: 22g

Korean Spicy Pork

Prep. Time: 5 minutes / Cook Time: 10 minutes / Serves: 4

Ingredients:

- 2 Lbs. Pork, Cut Into ⅛-Inch Slices
- 1/2 Cup Soy Sauce
- 5 Cloves Garlic, Minced
- 3 Tbsp. Minced Green Onion
- 1 Yellow Onion, Sliced
- 2 Tbsp. Sesame Seeds
- 3 Tsp. Black Pepper
- 1/2 Cup Brown Sugar
- 3 Tbsp. Gochujang (Korean Red Chili Paste)

Directions:

1. Mix all the ingredients together in a covered glass bowl or resealable bag and refrigerate for several hours to overnight.
2. Heat the griddle grill to high, and grill the pork for 2–3 minutes per side until it is cooked through.
3. Serve immediately on rice or lettuce leaves with soy and/or kimchi.

Nutrition value per serving:

Calories: 120, Fats: 5g, Protein: 12g, carbs

Beef Bulgogi

Prep. Time: 12 hours / Cook Time: 30 minutes / Serves: 4

Ingredients:

- 2 lbs. flank steak
- 1/2 cup soy sauce
- 1/2 cup brown sugar
- 2 Tbsp. chopped green onion
- 4 cloves garlic, minced
- 2 Tbsps. sesame seeds
- 2 Tbsps. sesame oil
- 2 tsps. black pepper

Directions:

1. Mix all of the ingredients together in a bowl or bag and refrigerate for several hours to overnight.
2. Heat the griddle grill to high, and grill the steak for several minutes per side until it is at your preferred doneness.
3. Let rest for several minutes before slicing and serving.

Nutrition value per serving:

Calories: 339kcal, Carbs: 7g, Fats: 17g, Protein: 35g

Hibachi Steak

Prep. Time: 5 minutes / Cook Time: 5 minutes / Serves: 4

Ingredients:

- 2 Lbs. Tri-Tip Beef, Cut Into 1/8-Inch Slices
- 1/2 Cup Teriyaki Sauce
- 1 Tsp. Fresh Grated Ginger
- 2 Cloves Garlic, Minced
- 1/4 Cup Brown Sugar
- 2 Tbsp. Worcestershire Sauce
- 3 Tsp. Black Pepper

Directions:

1. Mix all the ingredients together in a covered bowl or resealable bag, and refrigerate for several hours to overnight.
2. Heat the griddle grill to high and grill for about 1 minute per side until cooked through.
3. Let rest for several minutes before serving.

Nutrition value per serving:

Calories: 451, Carbs: 2g, Fats: 32g, Protein: 37g

Moroccan Lamb Kabobs

Prep. Time: 10 minutes / Cook Time: 10 minutes / Serves: 4

Ingredients:

- 2 Lbs. Lamb, Cut Into 1/8-Inch Strips
- 6 Garlic Cloves, Minced
- 1/2 Cup Olive Oil
- 1 Tbsp. Coriander
- 2 Tsp. Cumin
- Zest And Juice Of 2 Lemons
- 2 Tbsp. Fresh Mint, Chopped
- 3 Tsp. Salt
- 2 Tsp. Black Pepper
- Apricot Jam

Directions:

1. Mix all of the ingredients except for the apricot jam together, and place in the refrigerator for several hours to overnight.
2. Put all the lamb pieces onto skewers, leaving space between the pieces.
3. Heat the griddle grill to high, and grill the skewers for 3–4 minutes per side until cooked through.
4. Brush the apricot jam on the lamb, and grill for less than 1 minute on each side to set the glaze.
5. Let the meat relax for 5 minutes before serving.

Nutrition value per serving:

Calories: 149, Carbs: 3g, Fats: 9g, Protein: 12g

Parmesan Garlic Beef

Prep. Time: 3 hours / Cook Time: 10 minutes / Serves: 4

Ingredients:

- 2 Lbs. Sirloin Beef, Cut Into 1-Inch Cubes
- 6 Garlic Cloves, Finely Minced
- 1/4 Cup Olive Oil
- Sea Salt To Taste
- 1/4 Cup Grated Parmesan

Directions:

1. Mix the ingredients together and place them in a covered bowl or bag in the fridge for 3 hours to overnight.
2. Place the beef chunks onto skewers.
3. Heat the griddle grill to high, and grill for about 3 minutes per side, sprinkling each side with parmesan. Grill for a few minutes more until it's done to the point you like it.
4. Let the meat relax for several minutes before serving.

Nutrition value per serving:

Calories: 175.2, Carbs: 75g, Fats: 4g, Protein: 30.7g

Chapter 7: Poultry Recipes

Bacon Chipotle Chicken Panini

Prep. Time: 10 minutes / Cook Time: 5 minutes / Serves: 1

Ingredients:

- 2 Slices Sourdough Bread
- 1/4 Cup Caesar Salad Dressing
- 1 Cooked Chicken Breast, Diced
- 1/2 Cup Shredded Cheddar Cheese
- 1 Tbsp. Bacon Bits
- 1-1/2 Tsps. Chipotle Chili Powder, Or To Taste
- 2 Tbsps. Softened Butter

Directions:

1. Preheat the Griddle Grill to Medium-High with unit closed.
2. Spread the salad dressing on one side of both pieces of bread. Then top the dressing side of one piece of bread with chicken, then cheese, then bacon, and finally chipotle chili powder.
3. Place the other piece of bread with the dressing side down on top. Butter the other side of both pieces of bread.
4. Cook the Panini for 5 minutes, checking halfway through. The bread should be brown, and the cheese should be melted.

Nutrition value per serving:

Calories 407; Fat13 g; Carbs 4 g; Protein 10g

Buffalo Chicken Panini

Prep. Time: 30 minutes / Cook Time: 4 minutes / Serves: 4

Ingredients:

- 2 cups shredded cooked chicken
- 1 large sweet onion, sliced
- 8 slices seedless rye
- 1/4 lb. thinly sliced Swiss cheese, about 8 slices
- 1/4 cup blue cheese dressing
- 1 cup mayonnaise
- 1 cup buffalo hot sauce
- 2 tbsps. unsalted butter
- blue cheese dressing

Directions:

1. Melt the butter in a large skillet on medium heat. Add the onions and cook for about 20 minutes.
2. Mix the buffalo sauce and mayonnaise in a medium bowl and toss with the chicken.
3. Put a slice of cheese on a piece of bread then the chicken, the onions and top with another slice of cheese and top with another piece of bread. Repeat the process with the remaining sandwiches. Spread the butter on the top and bottom of the sandwich
4. Preheat the Griddle Grill to Medium-High with unit closed.
5. Cook the sandwiches for 4 minutes, and make sure to check halfway through. The bread should be brown, and the cheese should be melted. Serve the sandwiches with a side of the blue cheese dressing.

Nutrition value per serving:

Calories 387 Fat 11.3g, protein 9g, carbs 7g

Spicy Chicken Breasts

Prep. Time: 15 minutes / Cook Time: 15 minutes / Serves: 4

Ingredients:

- Chicken breasts – 4, skinless & boneless.
- Red pepper flakes – 1 tbsp.
- Chili powder – 1 tbsp.
- Brown sugar – 6 tbsps.
- BBQ sauce – 6 tbsps.
- Pineapple juice – 1 cup.

Directions:

1. Add chicken breasts into the zip-lock bag.
2. Mix together pineapple juice, BBQ sauce, brown sugar, chili powder, and red pepper flakes and pour over chicken breasts. Seal zip-lock bag and place in the refrigerator overnight.
3. Heat the griddle grill to a medium-high heat.
4. Place marinated chicken breasts on the hot grill and cook for 12-15 minutes or until done. Serve.

Nutrition value per serving:

Calories 407, Carbs 31.6g, Fat 11.5g, Protein 42.9g

Chicken Portobello Panini

Prep. Time: 15 minutes / Cook Time: 5 minutes / Serves: 4

Ingredients:

- 1 tbsp. olive oil
- 1 tbsp. red wine vinegar
- 1/2 tsp. Italian Seasoning Mix
- 1/2 tsp. salt
- 1/4 tsp. coarsely ground black pepper
- 1 garlic clove, pressed
- 2 large Portobello mushroom caps
- 2 slices (1/2" thick) large white onion
- 1 cup (4 ounces) grated Provolone cheese
- 2 plum tomatoes, sliced
- 8 slices (3/4" thick) Italian bread
- 1 cup shredded roasted chicken

Directions:

1. Preheat the griddle grill on medium heat for 5 minutes. Then place the onions and the mushrooms in the grill. Allow them to cook for about 4 to 6 minutes, making sure to flip halfway through. Cut the onions in half and the mushrooms into thin slices.
2. Brush what's going to be the outside of the bread with olive oil. Top half the pieces of bread with a layer cheese, then, chicken, then mushrooms, then onions, then tomatoes, and a second layer of cheese. Top with another piece of bread making sure the olive oil side is on the outside.
3. Preheat the Griddle Grill to Medium-High.
4. Cook the sandwiches for 5 minutes, and make sure to flip halfway through. The bread should be brown, and the cheese should be melted.

Nutrition value per serving:

Calories 252, Fat 10.3g, carbs 5.5g, protein 8g

Hawaiian Chicken

Prep. Time: 12 hours / Cook Time: 10 minutes / Serves: 5

Ingredients:

- 8 slices Italian bread
- 8 fresh basil leaves
- 8 thinly sliced tomatoes
- 16 slices of Black Pepper Turkey Breast
- 4 pieces of mozzarella cheese
- 4 tbsps. mayonnaise
- Olive oil

Directions:

1. Add chicken into the large zip-lock bag. Mix together ginger, garlic, brown sugar, pineapple juice, and soy sauce and pour over chicken.
2. Seal zip-lock bag shake well and place in the refrigerator overnight.
3. Heat griddle grill to a medium heat.
4. Remove chicken from the zip-lock bag and set aside. Pour marinade in a medium saucepan and simmer for 5-10 minutes.
5. Place chicken on the hot grill and brush with the hot marinade and grill until chicken is cooked or until the internal temperature of the chicken reaches 165 F. Serve.

Nutrition value per serving:

Calories 523, Carbs 53g, Fat 23g, Protein 27g

Southwestern Turkey Panini

Prep. Time: 15 minutes / Cook Time: 5 minutes / Serves: 4

Ingredients:

- 1 medium Avocado peeled and seeded
- 1/2 tbsp. Cilantro leaves finely chopped
- 1/2 tsp. Lime juice
- Salt to taste
- Chipotle mayonnaise (store bought or homemade)
- 4 slices large Sourdough bread
- 8 slices Colby Jack Cheese
- 8 slices Blackened Oven Roasted Turkey Breast
- 4 slices Tomato

Directions:

1. Preheat the Griddle Grill to Medium-High.
2. Mash and mix the avocado, lime and cilantro, and then salt and pepper to taste.
3. Spread the chipotle mayonnaise on one side of every piece of bread. On 2 pieces of bread with the mayonnaise side facing up place a layer of cheese, then turkey, then tomato, then avocado mixture, then turkey, and finally cheese again. Top with another piece of bread with the mayonnaise side touching the cheese.
4. Cook the sandwiches for 5 minutes, and make sure to check halfway through. The bread should be toasted, and the cheese should be melted.

Nutrition value per serving:

Calories 280, Fat 10.5g, Carbs 43g, Protein 13g

Grilled Chicken Drumsticks

Prep. Time: 40 minutes / Cook Time: 10 minutes / Serves: 6

Ingredients:

- Chicken drumsticks – 12.
- Mustard – 1 tsp.
- White vinegar – 2 tbsps.
- Soy sauce – 1 cup, low-sodium.
- Brown sugar –1/2 cup.
- Granulated sugar – 1/2 cup.
- Tomato sauce – 15 oz.

Directions:

1. Add all ingredients except chicken to a large pot and heat over a medium-high heat.
2. Stir well and bring mixture to boil. Add chicken drumsticks and turn heat to medium-low.
3. Cover and simmer for about 20-30 minutes or until chicken is cooked. Remove chicken drumsticks to a plate.
4. Heat the griddle grill to a high heat and oil grates. Place chicken drumsticks on the hot grill and cook for 3-5 minutes.
5. Turn chicken drumsticks and cook for 3-5 minutes more. Serve.

Nutrition value per serving:

Calories 208, Carbs 21g, Fat 7g, Protein 15g

Honey Jalapeno Chicken

Prep. Time: 20 minutes / Cook Time: 20 minutes / Serves: 4

Ingredients:

- 1-1/2 lbs. Chicken thighs, skinless and boneless.
- 1 tsp. Garlic, crushed.
- 1 Jalapeno pepper, minced.
- 3 tbsps. Fresh lime juice
- 3 tbsps. Honey
- 3 tbsps. Olive oil
- 1 tsp. Kosher salt

Directions:

1. Add chicken and remaining ingredients into the zip-lock bag. Seal bag and place in the refrigerator overnight.
2. Heat the griddle grill to a medium-high heat. Spray grill with cooking spray.
3. Remove chicken from the marinade and place on a hot grill and cook for 8-10 minutes on each side. Serve.

Nutrition value per serving:

Calories 415, Carbs 14g, Fat 19g, Protein 43g

Zesty Basil Crusted Chicken

Prep. Time: 15 minutes / Cook Time: 5 minutes / Serves: 4

Ingredients:

- Salt and pepper for taste
- 1 pound boneless, skinless chicken meat, cut into bite-sized pieces
- 1 red bell pepper, washed and diced
- 8 ounces mushrooms, cleaned and sliced
- 2 cups zucchini or other summer squash (washed, stemmed and sliced)
- 3 garlic cloves (minced or pressed)
- 8 ounces fresh basil (chopped)

Directions:

1. Preheat the Griddle Grill to High.
2. Season the chicken with salt and pepper for taste.
3. Add the chicken to the griddle, cooking on both sides until brown.
4. Pour in the rest of the ingredients and cook for 3 minutes.

Nutrition value per serving:

Calories 550, Fat 33g, Carbs 9g, Protein Fat 16g

Sizzling Southwestern Cheddar Chicken

Prep. Time: 20 minutes / Cook Time: 20 minutes / Serves: 4

Ingredients:

- 1 lb. Boneless skinless chicken breasts
- 4oz taco seasoning
- 1 tsp. Cayenne pepper
- Kosher salt
- 2 cloves minced garlic
- 1 chopped small red onion
- 2 chopped red bell peppers
- 15-oz. Can black beans (drained)
- 2 cups shredded cheddar
- 1/2 cup chopped fresh cilantro

Directions:

1. Preheat Griddle Grill to High.
2. Sprinkle the chicken with the taco seasoning, cayenne pepper and salt.
3. Add it to the griddle and cook for 6 minutes on each side. Take chicken out when done.
4. Next, add the rest of the ingredients and cook for 7 minutes.
5. Re-add chicken to the griddle and cook for 2 minutes with cheese mixture.
6. Garnish and serve.

Nutrition value per serving:

Calories 530 kcal, Fat 15 g, Carbs 9g, protein 4.5 g

Flavorful Grilled Chicken Wings

Prep. Time: 12 hours / Cook Time: 20 minutes / Serves: 6

Ingredients:

- Chicken wings – 3 lbs.
- Garlic – 1-1/2 tsps., minced.
- Fresh thyme leaves – 1 tbsp., chopped.
- Fresh parsley – 1 tbsp., chopped.
- Lemon zest – 2 tsps., grated.
- Soy sauce – 3 tbsps.
- Dijon mustard – 1 tbsp.
- Brown sugar – 3 tbsps.
- Olive oil –1/2 cup.
- Pepper – 3/4 tsp.
- Salt – 1 tsp.

Directions:

1. Add chicken wings into the zip-lock bag.
2. In a medium bowl, whisk together the remaining ingredients and pour over the chicken wings. Seal zip-lock bag and place in the refrigerator for 8 hours.
3. Heat the griddle grill to a medium-high heat.
4. Remove chicken wings from the marinade and place on a hot grill and cook for 10 minutes per side. Serve.

Nutrition value per serving:

Calories 313, Carbs 5g, Fat 14g, Protein 30g

Chapter 8: Seafood Recipes

Ahi Tuna

Prep. Time: 5 minutes / Cook Time: 13 minutes / Serves: 2

Ingredients:

- Ahi Steaks, Cut About 1.5 Inches Thick
- Soy Sauce
- Brown Sugar
- Toasted Sesame Seeds

Directions:

1. Preheat the griddle grill to the highest setting.
2. Drizzle the soy sauce followed by the brown sugar on both sides of the ahi steaks.
3. Roll the steaks in the sesame seeds.
4. Spray the grill with spray oil.
5. Grill the ahi steaks for 2–3 minutes per side.
6. Let the steaks relax for 5 minutes.
7. Slice thin and serve. Drizzle with more soy sauce if desired.

Nutrition value per serving:

calories 120kcal, fat 13g, carbs 7g, Protein 6.8g

Swordfish

Prep. Time: 5 minutes / Cook Time: 15 minutes / Serves: 4

Ingredients:

- Swordfish Fillets, Cut About 1.5 Inches Thick
- Olive Oil
- Sea Salt And Pepper To Taste

Directions:

1. Preheat the griddle grill to high.
2. Drizzle the fillets with olive oil and season with sea salt and black pepper.
3. Place on the grill and cook for 3 minutes per side.
4. Turn the grill down to medium and continue grilling for 5 minutes per side or until the sides of the swordfish are homogeneous in color.
5. Let the fish relax for 5 minutes before serving.

Nutrition value per serving:

Calories: 132, carbs 8g, Protein: 22 g, Fat: 4 g

Halibut

Prep. Time: 5 minutes / Cook Time: 7 minutes / Serves: 4

Ingredients:

- Halibut Fillets, Cut About 1 Inch Thick
- Olive Oil
- Sea Salt And Pepper
- Fresh Grated Parmesan Cheese
- Fresh Chopped Parsley
- Fresh Lemon Juice

Directions:

1. Brush the halibut fillets with the olive oil and sprinkle with the salt and pepper.
2. Preheat the griddle grill to high.
3. Spray the grill with spray oil, and immediately place the halibut on the heat.
4. Grill for 2 minutes per side.
5. Turn the grill down to medium, and grill for 2 minutes per side.
6. Sprinkle the halibut with the parmesan, and grill an additional minute before removing from the heat.
7. Sprinkle the fillets with parsley and lemon juice, and let it relax for 5 minutes before serving.

Nutrition value per serving:

Calories 223, carbs 10g, Fat 5g, Protein 42g

Salmon

Prep. Time: 5 minutes / Cook Time: 15 minutes / Serves: 4

Ingredients:

- Boneless Salmon Fillets, Scaled
- Olive Oil
- Sea Salt And Pepper To Taste

Directions:

1. Preheat the griddle grill to high.
2. Drizzle the fillets with olive oil and season with sea salt and black pepper.
3. Place on the griddle grill, and cook for 3 minutes per side.
4. Turn the grill down to medium and continue grilling for several minutes until the fillet is homogeneous in color and white is beginning to appear on top of the fillet.
5. Remove from heat, and let it rest for a few minutes before serving.

Nutrition value per serving:

Calories 170kcal, Fat 8g, carbs 15g, Protein 26g

Scallops

Prep. Time: 5 minutes / Cook Time: 10 minutes / Serves: 4

Ingredients:

- Large Fresh Bay Scallops
- Real Butter, Melted
- Sea Salt And Pepper To Taste

Directions:

1. Preheat the griddle grill to high.
2. Melt the butter, and set it aside so that it is ready for later.
3. Season the scallops with salt and pepper.
4. Spray the grill with spray oil, and immediately place the scallops on the heat. Brush the tops with butter.
5. Grill for 3–4 minutes per side, brushing with the butter again after flipping. The scallops are ready to turn when they pull away easily from the grill.
6. Brush the scallops again with the butter, and grill for an additional thirty seconds per side.
7. Let the scallops relax for 5 minutes before serving.

Nutrition value per serving:

Calories 1070, Carbs 240g, Fat 89g, Protein 77g

Shrimp

Prep. Time: 20 minutes / Cook Time: 5 minutes / Serves: 4

Ingredients:

- Large Raw Shrimp, Peeled And Mud Vein Removed
- Olive Oil
- Garlic Salt To Taste
- Fresh Lime Juice

Directions:

1. Preheat the griddle grill to high.
2. Place the shrimp on the skewers through the center in the same direction.
3. Brush with olive oil and sprinkle with garlic salt.
4. Place the skewers on the grill and cook for 2 minutes on each side or until the half toward the heat has turned pink and white.
5. Drizzle with the lime juice, and grill a few seconds per side.
6. Remove from heat and serve immediately.

Nutrition value per serving:

Calories 101, Fat 1.4g, carbs 6g, protein 10g

Hibachi Salmon

Prep. Time: 12 hours / Cook Time: 10 minutes / Serves: 4

Ingredients:

- 2 lbs. salmon fillets
- 1/2 cup teriyaki sauce
- 1 tsp. fresh grated ginger
- 2 cloves garlic
- 1/4 cup brown sugar
- 2 tsp. black pepper
- 1 Tbsp. maple syrup

Directions:

1. Mix all the ingredients together in a covered glass bowl or resealable bag, and refrigerate for several hours to overnight.
2. Heat the griddle grill to high, and grill the salmon fillets for 3–4 minutes per side until cooked through. Salmon should be homogeneous in color with white juice between the flakes.
3. Let rest for several minutes before serving.

Nutrition value per serving:

Calories 251, Carbs, 3g, Fat 13g, Protein 30g

Shrimp on the Barbie

Prep. Time: 20 minutes / Cook Time: 55 minutes / Serves: 4

Ingredients:

- 3 Lbs. Large Raw Shrimp, Peeled And Deveined
- 1/2 Lb. Butter, Melted
- 3 Cloves Garlic, Minced
- Zest And Juice Of 1 Lemon
- 2 Tsp. Sea Salt
- 2 Tsp. Black Pepper
- 1/4 Cup Grated Parmesan Cheese

Directions:

1. Place the shrimp on skewers.
2. Mix the remaining ingredients together and set in a bowl.
3. Heat the griddle grill to high and grill the shrimp, brushing with the butter mixture, for 2 minutes per side until they are cooked through. They will be solid in color with white and pink tones rather than blue and gray.
4. Serve with grilled summer vegetables, grilled yellow potatoes, or grilled corn (elote).

Nutrition value per serving:

Calories 325, Fat 20g, carbs 8g, protein 13.7g

Salmon Lime Burgers

Prep. Time: 10 minutes / Cook Time: 10 minutes / Serves: 2

Ingredients:

- 2 hamburger buns, sliced in half
- 1 tablespoon cilantro, fresh minced
- 1/8 teaspoon fresh ground pepper
- 1/2 lb. Salmon fillets, skinless, cubed
- 1/2 tablespoon grated lime zest
- 1/4 teaspoon sea salt, fine ground
- 1-1/2 garlic cloves, minced
- 1/2 tablespoon Dijon mustard
- 1-1/2 tablespoons shallots, finely chopped
- 1/2 tablespoon honey
- 1/2 tablespoon soy sauce

Directions:

1. Mix all of your ingredients in a mixing bowl, except the hamburger buns.
2. Make 2 burger patties that are 1/2-inch thick with this mixture.
3. Preheat your griddle grill on the medium temperature setting.
4. Once your grill is preheated, place the 2 patties on the grill.
5. Grill your patties for 5 minutes per side. Serve on warm buns and enjoy!

Nutrition value per serving:

Calories 220, Fat: 15g, Protein: 16g, carbs 6g

Pesto Pistachio Shrimp

Prep. Time: 40 minutes / Cook Time: 10 minutes / Serves: 4

Ingredients:

- 1-1/2 lb. Uncooked shrimp, peeled and deveined
- 2 tablespoons lemon juice
- 1/4 cup Parmesan cheese, shredded
- 1/4 teaspoon of sea salt
- 1/8 teaspoon black ground pepper
- 1/2 cup olive oil
- 1/2 cup parsley, fresh minced
- 1 garlic clove, peeled
- 1/3 cup pistachios, shelled
- 1/4 teaspoon grated lemon zest
- 3/4 cup arugula, fresh

Directions:

1. Begin by adding the olive oil, lemon zest, garlic clove, pistachios, parsley, arugula and lemon juice to a blender. Blend until smooth.
2. Add your Parmesan cheese, sea salt and pepper, then mix well.
3. Toss in your shrimp and allow to marinate in the fridge for 30 minutes.
4. Thread your shrimp onto skewers.
5. Preheat your griddle grill on the medium temperature setting.
6. Once preheated, add your skewers onto the grill and close lid.
7. Grill for 6 minutes. Rotate the skewers every 2 minutes. Cooking skewers in batches. Serve and enjoy!

Nutrition value per serving:

Calories: 293, Fat: 16g, Carbs: 5.2g, Protein: 34.2g

Lime Ginger Salmon

Ingredients:

- 1 teaspoon onion, finely chopped
- 1/4 teaspoon sea salt
- 1 teaspoon ginger root, fresh minced
- 1 tablespoon rice vinegar
- 1 garlic clove, minced
- 2 teaspoons sugar
- 1/8 cup lime juice
- 1 cucumber, peeled and chopped
- 1/6 cup cilantro, fresh chopped
- 1/4 teaspoon coriander, ground
- 1/4 teaspoon ground pepper

Salmon:

- 5 (6-ounces) salmon fillets
- 1/4 teaspoon of sea salt
- 1/4 teaspoon freshly ground black pepper
- 1/6 cup ginger root, minced
- 1/2 tablespoon olive oil
- 1/2 tablespoon lime juice

Directions:

1. Begin by blending the first 11 ingredients in a blender until smooth.
2. Season your salmon fillets with olive oil, lime juice, ginger, salt and pepper.
3. Preheat your griddle grill to the medium temperature setting.
4. Once your grill is preheated, place 2 salmon fillets on the grill.
5. Grill it for 4 minutes per side.
6. Cook the remaining fillets in the same manner.
7. Serve salmon fillets with prepared sauce and enjoy!

Nutrition value per serving:

Calories: 457 Fat: 19.1g Carbs; 18.9g Protein: 32.5g

Seafood Stuffed Sole

Prep. Time: 10 minutes / Cook Time: 14 minutes / Serves: 2

Ingredients:

- 1/4 cup shrimp, cooked, peeled and chopped
- 1 tablespoon lemon juice
- 2 tablespoons butter, melted, divided
- 3/4 cup cherry tomatoes
- 1 tablespoon chicken broth
- 1/2 can (6-ounces) crabmeat, drained
- 1/2 teaspoon parsley, fresh minced
-

- 1 tablespoon whipped cream cheese
- 1/2 teaspoon grated lemon zest
- 2 tablespoons breadcrumbs
- 1 teaspoon chive, minced
- 2 (6-ounces) sole fish fillets, cut from the side with gutted and cleaned
- 1/4 teaspoon black ground pepper

Directions:

1. Mix your cream cheese, cram, shrimp, garlic, lemon zest, parsley, 2 tablespoons butter and breadcrumbs in a mixing bowl.
2. Stuff each fillet with 1/4 of this mixture and secure the ends with toothpicks.
3. Mix lemon juice, tomatoes, salt and pepper in a different bowl.
4. Place your stuffed fillets in a foil sheet and top with the tomato mixture.
5. Cover and seal the fillets in foil.
6. Preheat your griddle grill on the medium temperature setting.
7. Once your grill is preheated, place 2 sealed fillets on the grill.
8. Grill it for 7 minutes per side. Serve and Enjoy!

Nutrition value per serving:

Calories: 248 Fat: 2.7g Carbs: 31.4g Protein: 24.9g

Chapter 9: Vegan & Vegetarian Recipes

Grilled Yellow Potatoes

Prep. Time: 10 minutes / Cook Time: 50 minutes / Serves: 4

Ingredients:

- Yellow Potatoes
- Olive Oil
- Sea Salt And Black Pepper To Taste
- Paprika

Directions:

1. Slice the potatoes in half lengthwise, and place them into a large bag or bowl.
2. Drizzle them with olive oil, and stir or shake to coat the potatoes.
3. Add the salt, pepper, and paprika to taste, and stir or shake until completely combined.
4. Preheat the griddle grill to medium, and spray it with oil.
5. Place the potatoes sliced-side down, and grill for several minutes or until you can see grill marks and they feel tender on the cut side.
6. Turn the potatoes over and grill until they are tender through.
7. Remove from heat and serve.

Nutrition value per serving:

Calories 280, Fat 11g, carbs 8g, Protein 4g

Grilled Summer Squash

Prep. Time: 10 minutes / Cook Time: 10 minutes / Serves: 12

Ingredients:

- 1 Summer Squash
- 2 tbsps. Olive Oil
- Sea Salt To Taste

Directions:

1. Slice the squash in half lengthwise. Brush the squash with the olive oil and season with salt.
2. Heat the griddle grill to medium heat, and set the squash cut-side down. Cook for 5 minutes per side until it is tender.
3. Remove from heat and serve.

Nutrition value per serving:

Calories 74, Fat 5.4g, protein 10g, carbs 6.1g

Elote (Spanish Corn on the Cob)

Prep. Time: 10 minutes / Cook Time: 10 minutes / Serves: 4-6

Ingredients:

- Corn On The Cob
- Olive Oil
- Sea Salt To Taste
- Mayonnaise
- Tepín Chili Lime Salt*
- Grated Parmesan Cheese

Directions:

1. Remove the corn from the husk.
2. Brush with olive oil and sprinkle with sea salt.
3. Heat the griddle grill to high, and grill for several minutes, turning the corn over as needed. The corn is done when it begins to wrinkle.
4. Brush with mayo and sprinkle with chili lime salt and parmesan cheese to serve.

* Tepín is sold at most Latin markets. You can also substitute with creole seasoning.

Nutrition value per serving:

Calories 164.8, Fat 8.1 g, carbs 6g, protein 13g

Grilled Eggplant Napoleon

Prep. Time: 10 minutes / Cook Time: 5 minutes / Serves: 4

Ingredients:

- 1 Eggplant sliced lengthwise into half inch slices
- Olive Oil brushed
- Salt to taste
- Heirloom Tomatoes sliced thin
- Lemon squeezed
- Balsamic Vinegar drizzled
- Fresh Basil garnished
- Haloumi cheese sliced to 1/4 inch thick and grilled

Directions:

1. Slice the eggplant thin lengthwise and brush with the olive oil and season with the sea salt.
2. Slice the Halloumi to 1/4 inch and grill on high for one minute per side
3. Turn the griddle grill on high and grill the eggplant for several minutes per side until the grill marks are prevalent.
4. Layer with the eggplant with grilled halloumi, and sliced tomatoes. Squeeze the lemon juice over the top, drizzle the balsamic vinegar, and garnish with slightly torn fresh basil.

Nutrition value per serving:

Calories 232.4, Fat 6.7 g, carbs 9g, Protein 11.2 g

Grilled Sweet Potatoes

Prep. Time: 5 minutes / Cook Time: 10 minutes / Serves: 4

Ingredients:

- Sweet Potatoes
- Olive Oil
- Sea Salt To Taste

Directions:

1. Slice the sweet potatoes in half lengthwise.
2. Brush the entire sweet potato with olive oil and season liberally with sea salt.
3. Heat the griddle grill to high, and grill the sweet potatoes cut-side down for 5–7 minutes. Turn them over and grill on medium heat until the sweet potatoes are tender through.
4. Let the potatoes relax for several minutes before serving.

Nutrition value per serving:

Calories 160.3, Fat 10.7 g, carbs 6g, Protein 1.1 g

Grilled Artichokes with Honey Dijon

Prep. Time: 45 minutes / Cook Time: 30 minutes / Serves: 4-6

Ingredients:

- 6 whole artichokes
- 1/2 gallon water
- 3 Tbsp. sea salt
- olive oil
- sea salt to taste
- 1/4 cup raw honey
- 1/4 cup boiling water
- 3 Tbsp. Dijon mustard

Directions:

1. Cut the artichokes in half lengthwise top to bottom.
2. Mix the 3 tablespoons of sea salt and water together. Place the artichokes in the brine for 30 minutes to several hours before cooking.
3. Heat the griddle grill to medium.
4. Remove the artichokes from the brine, drizzle with olive oil on the cut side, and season with sea salt.
5. Grill for 15 minutes on each side, cut side down first.
6. Turn the grill down to low, and turn the artichokes cut-side down while you mix the honey, boiling water, and Dijon.
7. Turn the artichokes back over, and brush the Dijon mix well over the cut side until it is all absorbed.
8. Serve alongside a protein like salmon, beef, pork, or chicken, or with rice or potatoes for a vegetarian option.

Nutrition value per serving:

Calories 601kcal, Fat 57g, Protein 8g, Carbs 21g

Grilled BBQ Tofu

Prep. Time: 3 hours / Cook Time: 20 minutes / Serves: 2-3

Ingredients:

- Firm Tofu
- Olive Oil
- Sea Salt To Taste
- Bbq Sauce

Directions:

1. Cut the tofu into 1-inch strips, and freeze them.
2. Place the frozen tofu strips on a cookie sheet that is covered with paper towels. Layer more paper towels on top of the tofu, and place another cookie sheet on top. Add weight to press the liquid out of the tofu as it thaws.
3. Once the tofu is completely thawed, brush the strips with olive oil and sea salt.
4. Heat the griddle grill to high, and grill the strips for 10 minutes per side.
5. Brush with BBQ sauce, and return them to the grill for a couple of minutes to set the sauce before serving.

Nutrition value per serving:

Calories 435.7, Fat 32.2 g, carbs 18g, protein 21g

Coleslaw

Prep. Time: 15 minutes / Cook Time: 30 minutes / Serves: 4

Ingredients:

For the coleslaw

- 1 head shredded green cabbage
- 1 cup shredded carrots
- 2 thinly sliced scallions
- 1 head shredded purple cabbage

For the dressing

- 1/8 cup white wine vinegar
- 1 tbsp. celery seed
- 1-1/2 cups mayonnaise
- 1 tsp. sugar
- Salt and pepper, to taste

Directions:

1. Set the griddle grill on preheat with the temperature reaching 180 degrees F
2. Now place both carrots and cabbage on a sheet tray and then place it on the grill grates directly
3. Grill it for approx 25 minutes.
4. Remove it from the grill and immediately keep it in the refrigerator so as to cool
5. For the dressing
6. Take a small bowl and mix and the ingredients in it
7. Now, take a large bowl and place cabbage and carrot in it.
8. Pour the dressing over it and stir to coat thoroughly
9. Transfer to a serving dish and sprinkle scallions
10. Serve and enjoy

Nutrition value per serving:

Calories 83, Fat 3.1 g, protein 29g, carbs 14.9 g

Roasted Tomatoes With Hot Pepper Sauce

Prep. Time: 3 minutes / Cook Time: 120 minutes / Serves: 4-6

Ingredients:

- 2 lbs. tomatoes; Roma fresh
- 1 lb. spaghetti
- 2 tbsps. chopped garlic
- 1/2 cup olive oil
- 3 tbsps. chopped parsley
- Salt, hot pepper and black pepper, to taste

Directions:

1. Set the griddle grill to preheat and push the temperature to 400 degrees F.
2. Now take the tomatoes, wash them thoroughly and cut them into halves; lengthwise.
3. Place it on a baking dish while making sure that the cut side faces upwards
4. Sprinkle it with chopped parsley, salt, black pepper, and garlic.
5. Also, put 1/4 cup of olive oil over them
6. Now place it on the grill for 1-1/2 hour
7. The tomatoes will shrink, and the skin is likely to get slightly blackened
8. Now remove the tomatoes from the baking dish and place it on the food processor and puree it well
9. Drop the pasta into the boiling salt water and cook it until it turns tender
10. Drain and toss it immediately with the pureed tomatoes mix
11. Now add the leftover 1/4 cup of raw olive oil along with crumbled hot pepper as per taste
12. Toss well and serve

Nutrition value per serving:

Calories 45, Fat 1g, Carbs 8g, Protein 2g

Grilled Zucchini Squash Spears

Prep. Time: 15 minutes / Cook Time: 15 minutes / Serves: 6

Ingredients:

- 4 midsized zucchini
- 2 springs thyme with the leaves pulled out
- 1 tbsp. sherry vinegar
- 2 tbsps. olive oil
- Salt and pepper as per your taste

Directions:

1. Take the zucchini and cut off the ends
2. Now cut each of them in a half and then cut every half into thirds
3. Take all the leftover ingredients in a midsized zip lock bag and then add spears to it
4. Toss it and mix well so that it coats the zucchini
5. Start the griddle grill to preheat to medium high
6. Remove the spears from the bag and place them directly on the grill grate. Make sure that the side faces downwards
7. Cook for 3 to 4 minutes per side until you can see the grill starts popping up and the zucchini should become tender too
8. Remove from the grill and add more thyme leaves if needed
9. Serve and enjoy

Nutrition value per serving:

Calories 235, Carbs 21g, Fat 16g, Protein 8g

Chapter 10: Game Recipes

Duck Poppers

Prep. Time: 20 minutes / Cook Time: 20 minutes / Serves: 4

Ingredients:

- 8 – 10 pieces bacon, cut event into same-sized pieces measuring 4 inches each
- 3 duck breasts; boneless and with skin removed and sliced into strips measuring 1/2 inches
- Sriracha sauce
- 6 de-seeded jalapenos, with the top cut off and sliced into strips

Directions:

1. Wrap the bacon around one trip of pepper and one slice of duck
2. Secure it firmly with the help of a toothpick
3. Fire the griddle grill on low flame and keep this wrap and grill it for half an hour until the bacon turns crisp
4. Rotate often to ensure even cooking
5. Serve with sriracha sauce

Nutrition value per serving:

Calories 163.8; fat 12g, protein 8.9 g; carbs 2 g.

Wild Mushroom Asiago Pizza

Prep. Time: 10 minutes / Cook Time: 1 hour / Serves: 6

Ingredients:

- 3 Portobello Mushrooms
- 10 Shiitake Mushrooms
- 10 Oyster Mushrooms
- 1 Pizza Dough, Thin Crust
- 16 Slices Asiago Cheese
- 3 Tbsp. Grana Padano Cheese, Grated

Directions:

1. Use the Griddle grill to tenderize the mushrooms. Chop and set aside.
2. Preheat the oven to 400° F.
3. Arrange dough to fit onto the Grill Pan. Grill both sides, then flip again.
4. Distribute both cheeses, chopped mushrooms, and garlic over the pizza. Sprinkle with truffle salt. Drizzle with olive oil.
5. Finish cooking in the oven for about 10 minutes.
6. Slice pizza before serving with your favorite side dishes.

Nutrition value per serving:

Calories 191, Carbs 18g, Fat 9g, Protein 10g

Flounder Spaghetti

Prep. Time: 10 minutes / Cook Time: 30 minutes / Serves: 6

Ingredients:

- 1 lb. spaghetti
- 1 lb. flounder fillet
- 4 cloves garlic, sliced 1/4 cup extra virgin olive oil
- 1/2 cup parsley, chopped
- 1/2 tsp. red pepper flakes

Directions:

1. Cook spaghetti according to the box directions.
2. Griddle grill the flounder on medium heat to desired doneness.
3. In a separate pot, sauté the garlic in olive oil until lightly golden.
4. Add cooked pasta, parsley, red pepper flakes, and flounder to the pot. Season with salt and pepper.
5. Serve spaghetti with lemon wedges.

Nutrition value per serving:

Calories 270.2, Fat 10.7 g, carbs 8g, protein 18g

Cheddar Jalapeño Stuffed Burger

Prep. Time: 10 minutes / Cook Time: 20 minutes / Serves: 6

Ingredients:

- Burger Mixture
- 2 lb. ground beef
- 1 tsp. sea salt
- 1 tsp. ground black pepper
- 3 tbsp. cilantro, chopped ½ small onion, peeled & minced
- 1 jalapeño, seeded & chopped

Directions:

1. Combine ground beef, sea salt, pepper, cilantro, onion, and jalapeño.
2. Divide ground beef mixture into 4 balls. Stuff each ball with a chunk of cheddar.
3. Rub burgers with olive oil. Griddle grill it for about 5 minutes per side or to desired doneness.
4. Top burgers with sliced cheddar.
5. Spread each roll with margarine. Grill to desired doneness. Serve burgers topped with pickled jalapeños.

Nutrition value per serving:

526.1 calories; 19g fat; 27.2 g protein; 24.4 g carbs

Skirt Steak & Tomato Tapenade Sandwich

Prep. Time: 1 hour / Cook Time: 20 minutes / Serves: 6

Ingredients:

- 1 lb. skirt steak
- 1 shallot, peeled & minced
- 3 tbsp. balsamic vinegar 1/4 cup olive oil 1/2 tsp. sea salt

Directions:

1. In a shallow pan, marinate steak with shallots, balsamic vinegar, olive oil, sea salt, and pepper for 1 hour.
2. Combine tapenade ingredients in a bowl. Set aside.
3. Griddle grill the steak to desired temperature. Let rest 10 minutes before slicing.
4. Assemble sliced steak and tapenade open-face on focaccia. Serve with your favorite side dish.

Nutrition value per serving:

Calories: 700 Cal, Fat: 51g Carbs: 20 g Protein: 44 g.

Mac & Cheese Quesadilla

Prep. Time: 10 minutes / Cook Time: 20 minutes/ Serves: 4

Ingredients:

- 2 cups heavy cream
- 2 cups cheddar, shredded
- 1 tbsp. cornstarch
- 2 tbsp. butter
- 2 cups elbow macaroni, cooked
- 4 (8-in.) tortillas
- 12 slices American cheese, yellow 1/2 tsp. sea salt 1/2 tsp. ground black pepper

Directions:

1. In a pot, bring heavy cream to a boil.
2. Combine cheddar and cornstarch in a bowl.
3. Add butter and cheddar cheese mixture to the hot cream. Stir until creamy.
4. Stir in macaroni until well incorporated. Set aside to cool.
5. Arrange 1 tortilla on the Griddle Grill Pan. Top with 3 slices American cheese, 1 cup mac and cheese, and 3 more slices American cheese. Season with salt and pepper. Complete with a second tortilla.
6. Grill quesadilla until cheese is melted and tortilla is cooked.
7. Repeat to make the second quesadilla.

Nutrition value per serving:

Calories: 1020 kcal Fat 49g Carbs: 111 g Protein: 34g

Flank Steak with Balsamic Onion Dressing

Prep. Time: 10 minutes / Cook Time: 20 minutes / Serves: 4

Ingredients:

- 1 Flank Steak
- 1 Tsp. Sea Salt
- 1 Tsp. Ground Black Pepper
- 2 Tbsp. Olive Oil
- Balsamic Onion Dressing

Directions:

1. Rub flank steak with sea salt, pepper, and olive oil.
2. Mix dressing ingredients together.
3. Remove onions from dressing and grill until tender. Cut onions into quarters before returning to the dressing.
4. Griddle grill the steaks to desired temperature.
5. Let steaks rest before slicing. Drizzle with dressing before serving with your favorite side dish.

Nutrition value per serving:

Calories278.8, Protein 96g Carbs 30g Fat 28g

BBQ Chicken Pizza

Prep. Time: 10 minutes / Cook Time: 30 minutes / Serves: 6

Ingredients:

Tandoori Marinade

- 2 chicken breasts 1/2 cup BBQ sauce
- 1 red onion, peeled & sliced
- 2 tbsp. olive oil
- 1 pizza dough, thin crust
- 1 cup shredded cheddar
- 4 scallions, chopped

Directions:

1. In a bowl, combine 1/4 cup BBQ sauce with chicken. Grill it using Griddle Grill until fully cooked. Allow to cool, then chop into pieces.
2. Preheat the grill to medium high.
3. Toss the onions with olive oil. Using the Griddle grill, grill it to desired doneness.
4. Arrange dough to fit onto the Griddle Grill Pan. Grill one side of the pizza, then flip. Brush cooked side with remaining BBQ sauce. Top with cheddar cheese, red onion, and diced chicken.
5. Finish cooking in the oven for about 10 minutes.
6. Slice and sprinkle with scallions before serving.

Nutrition value per serving:

Calories: 350 kcal Fat: 13g Carbs: 41g Protein: 19g

Margherita Pizza

Prep. Time: 10 minutes / Cook Time: 25 minutes / Serves: 6

Ingredients:

- 1 Pizza Dough, Thin Crust
- 2 Tbsp. Basil Pesto
- 2 Tomatoes, Vine Ripe, Sliced
- 14 Slices Fresh Mozzarella
- 1 Clove Garlic, Peeled & Sliced Thin
- 1 Tbsp. Olive Oil

Directions:

1. Preheat the Griddle Pan on high heat.
2. Roll the pizza dough to fit onto the Pan. Cook on one side until golden.
3. Flip the dough. Spread the pesto on top followed by tomato slices, mozzarella slices, and garlic. Drizzle with olive oil.
4. Preheat the broiler.
5. Place the Pan under broiler to melt the cheese and toast the garlic.

Nutrition value per serving:

Calories: 260 Cal Fat: 13g Carbs: 23g Protein: 14g

Pesto Chicken Paillard

Prep. Time: 10 minutes / Cook Time: 1 hour / Serves: 6

Ingredients:

- 2 chicken breasts, sliced
- lengthwise & pounded 1/4 in. thick 4 tbsp. pesto
- Marinade 1/4 cup olive oil

Directions:

1. Combine chicken with marinade ingredients for 1-2 hours.
2. Using the Griddle Grill, grill the chicken until done. Chicken will cook quickly as it is very thin.
3. Remove chicken from the Grill Pan. Brush with pesto.
4. Combine salad ingredients in a large bowl. Toss.
5. Serve chicken over greens.

Nutrition value per serving:

Calories: 268 Cal Fat: 12 g Carbs: 1 g Protein: 24.1 g

Chapter 11: Desserts and Snacks

Grilled Peaches Cinnamon

Prep. Time: 10 minutes / Cook Time: 5 minutes / Serves: 4

Ingredients:

- 4 ripe peaches, halved and pitted
- 1/4 cup salted butter
- 1 teaspoon granulated sugar
- 1/4 teaspoon cinnamon

Directions:

1. Mix your sugar, butter and cinnamon in a bowl until smooth.
2. Preheat your griddle grill on the medium temperature setting.
3. Once your grill is preheated, place the peaches on the grill.
4. Grill it for 1 minute per side.
5. Serve the peaches with cinnamon butter on top and enjoy!

Nutrition value per serving:

Calories: 46.4 Fat: 0.1g Carbs: 54.7g Protein: 0.7g

Grilled Berry Cobbler

Prep. Time: 10 minutes / Cook Time: 20 minutes / Serves: 2

Ingredients:

- 2 cans (21-ounces) pie filling, raspberry flavor
- vanilla ice cream
- 1 (8-ounces) package of cake mix
- 1/2 cup olive oil
- 1-1/4 cups water

Directions:

1. Mix your cake mix with olive oil and water in a bowl until smooth.
2. Place a foil packet on the working surface along with pie filling.
3. Spread your cake mix on top of the pie filling.
4. Cover your foil packet and seal it.
5. Preheat your indoor grill on the medium temperature setting.
6. Once your grill is preheated, place the foil package on the grill.
7. Close the grill lid and set to "Bake Mode" for 20 minutes.
8. Serve with vanilla ice cream and enjoy!

Nutrition value per serving:

Calories: 319 Fat: 11.9g Carbs: 14.8g Protein: 5g

Marshmallow Stuffed Banana

Prep. Time: 10 minutes / Cook Time: 5 minutes / Serves: 1

Ingredients:

- 1 banana
- 1/4 cup chocolate chips
- 1/4 cup mini marshmallows

Directions:

1. Take the peeled banana and spread over a 12×12-inch foil sheet.
2. Slice a slit in the banana lengthwise and stuff the slit with chocolate chips and marshmallows.
3. Wrap some foil around the banana to seal it.
4. Prepare and preheat your Griddle Grill set to the medium temperature setting.
5. Once the grill is preheated and place the banana in the grill.
6. Grill each side for 5 minutes.
7. Unwrap your yummy treat, serve and enjoy it!

Nutrition value per serving:

Calories: 372 Fat: 11.8g Carbs: 45.8g Protein: 4g

Apricots with Brioche

Prep. Time: 10 minutes / Cook Time: 4 minutes / Serves: 4

Ingredients:

- 2 cups vanilla ice cream
- 2 tablespoons honey
- 4 slices brioches, diced
- 2 tablespoons sugar
- 2 tablespoons butter
- 8 ripe apricots

Directions:

1. Mix the halved apricots with sugar and butter.
2. Prepare and preheat your Griddle Grill on the medium temperature setting.
3. When your grill is preheated, put the brioche slices onto the grill.
4. Grill it for 1 minute per side.
5. Next, grill your apricots in the grill for 1 minute per side.
6. Top your brioche slices with honey, apricot slices, and a scoop of vanilla ice cream.
7. Serve your tasty dessert and enjoy it!

Nutrition value per serving:

Calories: 212 Fat: 9g Carbs: 28g Protein: 4g

Rum-Soaked Pineapple

Prep. Time: 10 minutes / Cook Time: 15 minutes / Serves: 6

Ingredients:

- 1/2 cup packed brown sugar
- 1/2 cup rum
- 1 teaspoon ground cinnamon
- 1 pineapple, cored and sliced
- cooking spray
- vanilla ice cream

Directions:

1. Mix the rum with brown sugar and cinnamon in a mixing bowl.
2. Pour this mixture over your pineapple rings and mix well.
3. Let the pineapple rings soak for about 15 minutes and flip the rings after 7 minutes.
4. Prepare and preheat your Griddle Grill setting it at a High-temperature setting.
5. Once your grill is preheated, place your pineapple rings on the grill.
6. Grill it for 4 minutes per side.
7. Serve your pineapple rings with a scoop of ice cream on top.

Nutrition value per serving:

Calories: 143.2 Fat: 0.4g Carbs: 21g Protein: 0.3g

Grilled Cinnamon S'mores Toast

Prep. Time: 10 minutes / Cook Time: 2 minutes / Serves: 4

Ingredients:

- 1/2 cup sugar
- 1 tbsp. cinnamon
- 4 slices bread 1/4 cup margarine
- 15 baby marshmallows
- 1 (4.4-oz.) chocolate bar

Directions:

1. Combine sugar and cinnamon in a bowl.
2. Spread margarine over one side of each slice of bread. Sprinkle with cinnamon and sugar mixture.
3. Arrange two slices of bread onto the Griddle Grill Pan, margarine side down. Cover each slice with marshmallows and half of the chocolate bar.
4. Top with remaining two slices of bread. Use Grill Press to cook on both sides, 3 minutes per side.
5. Serve alone or with a tall glass of milk!

Nutrition value per serving:

354.3 calories; 20g fat; 5.7 g protein; 54.1 g carbs

Chapter 12: Marinades, Rubs and Sauces

Easy BBQ Sauce

Prep. Time: 5 minutes / Cook Time: 15 minutes / Serves: 10

Ingredients:

- Brown sugar – 1-1/2 cups.
- Onion powder – 2 tsps.
- Paprika – 2 tsps.
- Worcestershire sauce – 1 tbsp.
- Apple cider vinegar –1/2 cup.
- Ketchup – 1-1/2 cups.
- Pepper – 1 tsp.
- Kosher salt – 2 tsps.

Directions:

1. Add all ingredients into a small saucepan and heat over a medium heat. Bring to boil. Turn heat to low and simmer for 15 minutes. Store and serve.

Nutrition value per serving:

Calories 167, Carbs 43g, Fat 3.4g, Protein 1g

BBQ White Sauce

Prep. Time: 5 minutes / Cook Time: 10 minutes / Serves: 16

Ingredients:

- Mayonnaise – 1-1/2 cups.
- Horseradish – 2 tsps.
- Worcestershire sauce – 1 tsp.
- Brown sugar – 1 tbsp.
- Spicy brown mustard – 1 tbsp.
- Onion powder –1/2 tsp.
- Garlic powder –1/2 tsp.
- Apple cider vinegar – 1/4 cup.
- Salt – 1 tsp.

Directions:

1. Add all ingredients into a mixing bowl and whisk until smooth. Pour sauce into an air-tight container and store in the refrigerator for up to 1 week.

Nutrition value per serving:

Calories 156, Carbs 1g, Fat 17g, Protein 1g

Perfect Honey BBQ Sauce

Prep. Time: 5 minutes / Cook Time: 15 minutes / Serves: 24

Ingredients:

- Ketchup – 1 cup.
- Onion powder – 1 tsp.
- Garlic powder – 1 tsp.
- Smoked paprika – 1 tsp.
- Honey – 2 tbsps.
- Apple cider vinegar –1/4 cup.
- Brown sugar –1/2 cup.
- Black pepper –1/2 tsp.
- Salt – 1 tsp.

Directions:

1. Add all ingredients into the saucepan and heat over a medium heat. Bring to boil. Turn heat to low and simmer for 15 minutes. Remove saucepan from heat and let it cool completely. Pour sauce into an air-tight container and store in the refrigerator for up to 2 weeks.

Nutrition value per serving:

Calories 35, Carbs 9g, Fat 1g, Protein 1g

Mango BBQ Sauce

Prep. Time: 5 minutes / Cook Time: 35 minutes / Serves: 12

Ingredients:

- Brown sugar –1/2 cup.
- Ground ginger – 1 tbsp.
- Smoked paprika – 1 tbsp.
- Ground mustard – 1 tbsp.
- Chili flakes – 2 tbsps.
- Honey – 3 tbsps.
- Apple cider vinegar – 3/4 cup.
- Tomato paste – 6 oz.
- Mango – 2 cups, chopped.
- Garlic cloves – 4, chopped.
- Habanero peppers – 4, diced.
- Small onion – 1, chopped.
- Olive oil – 1 tsp.
- Pepper & salt, to taste.

Directions:

1. Heat olive oil in a saucepan over a medium heat. Add peppers and onion and sauté for 5 minutes. Add garlic and sauté for a minute. Add remaining ingredients and stir until well combined. Bring to boil. Turn heat to low and simmer for 20-30 minutes. Remove saucepan from heat. Puree the sauce until smooth. Pour sauce into an air-tight container and store in the refrigerator.

Nutrition value per serving:

Calories 104, Carbs 23g, Fat 1g, Protein 1g

Peach BBQ Sauce

Prep. Time: 5 minutes / Cook Time: 20 minutes / Serves: 24

Ingredients:

- Ketchup –1/4 cup.
- Liquid smoke –1/4 tsp.
- Dry mustard –1/2 tsp.
- Chili powder – 1 tsp.
- Dijon mustard – 1 tbsp.
- Worcestershire sauce – 1 tbsp.
- Balsamic vinegar – 2 tbsps.
- Apple cider vinegar –1/4 cup.
- Soy sauce –1/4 cup.
- Tomato paste – 2 tbsps.
- Honey – 2 tbsps.
- Molasses – 2 tbsps.
- Brown sugar – 3/4 cup.
- Water – 1-1/2 cups.
- Frozen peaches – 1 lb.
- Bourbon – 4 tbsps.
- Jalapeno pepper – 2 tbsps., diced.
- Onion – 1 cup, diced.
- Olive oil – 2 tbsps.
- Black pepper –1/2 tsp.
- Kosher salt –1/2 tsp.

Directions:

1. Heat olive oil in a saucepan over medium heat.
2. Add jalapeno and onion and sauté for 3-4 minutes.
3. Add bourbon and cook for 1 minute.
4. Add 1 cup water and peaches and cook for 10 minutes. Remove saucepan from heat.
5. Pour pan contents into the food processor and process until smooth. Return blended mixture to the saucepan along with remaining ingredients and cook over medium heat for 5 minutes.
6. Remove saucepan from heat and let it cool completely. Pour sauce into an air-tight container and store in the refrigerator.

Nutrition value per serving:

Calories 55, Carbs 9.6g, Fat 1.2g, Protein 0.5g

Sweet & Spicy BBQ Sauce

Prep. Time: 5 minutes / Cook Time: 10 minutes / Serves: 40

Ingredients:

- Tomato sauce – 3-1/2 cups.
- White pepper–1/2 tsp.
- Red pepper flakes – 1 tsp.
- Ground mustard – 1 tbsp.
- Onion powder – 1 tbsp.
- Garlic powder – 1 tbsp.
- Paprika – 2 tbsps.
- Soy sauce – 3 tbsps.
- Worcestershire sauce – 3 tbsps.
- Molasses –1/2 cup.
- Brown sugar – 1 cup.

Directions:

1. Add tomato sauce, soy sauce, Worcestershire sauce, molasses, and brown sugar to a saucepan and stir well to combine.
2. Add paprika, white pepper, red pepper flakes, ground mustard, onion powder, and garlic powder and stir to combine.
3. Cook sauce over a medium heat. Bring to boil.
4. Turn heat to medium-low and simmer for 5 minutes. Remove saucepan from heat and let it cool completely.
5. Pour sauce into an air-tight container and store in the refrigerator.

Nutrition value per serving:

Calories 43, Carbs 11g, Fat 1g, Protein 1g

Conclusion

This outdoor cookbook has shown you how to use different ingredients to affect unique campfire-like tastes in dishes both sweet and savory.

How can you include these tasty recipes in your camping or grilling repertoire?

You can...

- Make camp fire hotcakes and breakfast burritos to wake up your camping crew. They are just as tasty as they sound.

- Learn to cook with heavy, cast-iron skillets and metal skewers, which are often used in camp fire cooking and backyard grilling. You can usually find them in camping or big-box stores in your local area.

- Enjoy making delectable seafood camping dishes, including salmon and shrimp. Fish is often on camping menus since you can sometimes catch your own. There are SO many ways to make it great.

- Make dishes featuring hot dogs and burgers, which are often used in both camping and backyard grilling.

- Make various types of desserts like blueberry cobbler and giant, soft cookies that will tempt your family's sweet tooth.

Have fun experimenting! Enjoy the results!

CPSIA information can be obtained
at www.ICGtesting.com
Printed in the USA
LVHW020005050121
675552LV00018B/671

9 781954 294547